My late mentor and colleague James Montgomery Boice had an exceptional gift for teaching the Bible. His exposition of James is one of his most practical books and has abiding relevance for Christian men and women today. Readers will gain a richer understanding of what it means to have a faith that really works.

Philip Graham Ryken,
Senior Minister, Tenth Presbyterian Church, Philadelphia

James Boice was one of the greatest Bible teachers of the twentieth century. This exposition of James is an outstanding help, displaying Boice's penetrating mind and easy to read style. I warmly commend it to pastors and all other Bible students.

Eric Alexander

SURE I BELIEVE – SO WHAT!

James Montgomery Boice

Christian Focus Publications

TO HIM
who is the source
of every good and perfect gift,
who does not change like shifting shadows

Dr James Montgomery Boice was the pastor of the Tenth Presbyterian Church, Philadelphia for over 32 years. In addition to his congregational work, he taught on the 'Bible Study Hour' radio broadcasts broadcast over 239 stations and around the world and was President of the Alliance of Confessing Evangelicals. A former chairman of the International Council on Biblical Inerrancy, he has written or contributed to over sixty books including Bible commentaries, doctrinal studies and devotional themes. Dr Boice died in his sleep on the 15th June 2000, from liver cancer that had been diagnosed just eight weeks earlier. When informing his congregation of his condition he asked them at one point 'If God does something in your life, would you change it? If you'd change it, you'd make it worse. It wouldn't be as good.' He is survived by his wife of 38 years, Linda; three daughters and three grandchildren.

© 1994 James Montgomery Boice
ISBN 1 85792 095 3

Published in 1994, reprinted in 2003
by
Christian Focus Publications
Geanies House, Fearn, Ross-shire,
IV20 1TW, Scotland

www.christianfocus.com

Cover design by Jonathan Williams

Printed and bound by
Cox & Wyman, Reading, Berkshire

Contents

STUDY QUESTIONS

Books by
James Montgomery Boice

Witness and Revelation in the Gospel of John
Philippians: An Expositional Commentary
The Sermon on the Mount
How to Live the Christian Life (originally, *How to Live It Up*)
Ordinary Men Called by God (originally, *How God Can Use Nobodies*)
The Last and Future World
The Gospel of John: An Expositional Commentary (5 volumes in one)
'Galatians' in the *Expositor's Bible Commentary*
Can You Run Away from God?
Our Sovereign God, editor
Our Savior God: Studies on Man, Christ and the Atonement, editor
Does Inerrancy Matter?
The Foundation of Biblical Authority, editor
Making God's Word Plain, editor
The Epistles of John
Genesis: An Expositional Commentary (3 volumes)
The Parables of Jesus
The Christ of Christmas
The Minor Prophets: An Expositional Commentary (2 volumes)
Standing on the Rock
The Christ of the Open Tomb
Foundations of the Christian Faith (4 volumes in one)
Christ's Call to Discipleship
Transforming Our World: A Call to Action, editor
Ephesians: An Expositional Commentary
Daniel: An Expositional Commentary
Joshua: We Will Serve the Lord
Nehemiah: Learning to Lead
The King Has Come
Romans (3 volumes)
Mind Renewal in a Mindless Age
Amazing Grace

PREFACE

The letter of James, the brother of our Lord, is not a popular book, which is surprising because it is so practical. We live in a practical age, so practical that most people are usually impatient with pure doctrine. Teach about justification, regeneration or some other largely theological theme, and they push you to get on to such subjects as 'How to Raise Your Children,' 'How to Have a Happy Marriage,' 'How to Apply Biblical Principles to the Work Place (and Get Rich Doing It),' and others like these. But if that is so and if James is a practical book, how is it that James is not more often read and thought about by Christians?

I think the problem is just that. It *is* practical, too practical in dealing with our own personal shortcomings, errors and sins! And it is so direct that we cannot easily dismiss or escape from James' teaching.

This reminds me of the story of a southern preacher, who was inveighing against sin. He preached against the sin of gambling, and a woman seated in the front row was obviously quite pleased. 'Preach it, brother,' she cried. Next the preacher denounced the sin of drunkenness. 'Amen!' the woman shouted. When he got to dancing and flirting she was ecstatic. 'Hallelujah,' she exclaimed.

Then the preacher mentioned gossiping, and the woman leaned over to her neighbor and said, 'Now he's not preachin', he's meddlin'.' I suspect that many people who begin to read James suspect before very long that he is indeed meddlin' with their sins and put the book down. After teaching that really is practical, it is always pretty nice to get back to 'just doctrine'.

But we can't do that, at least not if we are truly Christians. We cannot forget that at the beginning of Romans 8, after one of the most intensely doctrinal sections of the entire Bible, the Apostle Paul writes of the grace of God in salvation, concluding that it is so we might live holy lives, which is an immensely practical matter. Those verses say, 'Therefore, there is now no condemnation for those who are in Christ Jesus, because through Christ Jesus the law of the Spirit of life set me free from the law of sin and death. For what the law was powerless to do in that it was weakened by the sinful nature, God did by sending his own Son in the likeness of sinful man to be a sin offering. And so he condemned sin in sinful man, *in order that the righteous requirements of the law might be fully met in us*, who do not live according to the sinful nature but according to the Spirit' (Rom. 8:1-4).

Similarly, after the next doctrinal section of the same letter, chapters 9-11, Paul applies his doctrine, saying in pointed language, 'Therefore, I urge you, brothers, in view of God's mercy, *to offer your bodies as living sacrifices*, holy and pleasing to God – this is your spiritual act of worship. Do not conform any longer to the pattern of this world, but *be transformed by the renewing of your mind.* Then you will be able to test and approve what God's will is – his good, pleasing and perfect will' (Rom. 12:1, 2).

PREFACE

It is that way in nearly all Paul's letters. The great doctrinal sections are followed by pointed, practical applications of what he has been teaching.

James is not as overtly 'theological' as Paul, of course. He must have been a very 'down-to-earth' man, as we say. But his practical teaching is based on sound biblical doctrine, and his application of the Bible to daily living is something Paul would have himself heartily approved. The questions are: Will we approve? and, Will we profit from what we find in this epistle? I have tried to suggest the many areas in which we need to profit by the colloquial language of the chapter titles: 'Why Did God Let This Happen?' 'I Don't Want to Be a Fanatic,' 'My Friends Are Special,' 'Sure, I Believe, So What?,' 'At Least I'm No Hypocrite!,' 'It's His (Her) Fault,' 'How Much Insurance Do I Need?' 'Believe Me, Rich Is Better,' 'The Lord Helps Those Who ... ,' and 'Prayer Is for Weak People.'

These chapters were originally prepared as messages delivered to the evening congregations of Tenth Presbyterian Church. They were later broadcast as a special summer series for the Bible Study Hour radio network.

James Montgomery Boice
Philadelphia, Pennsylvania

1

WHY DID GOD LET THIS HAPPEN?
(James 1:1-18)

Consider it pure joy, my brothers, whenever you face trials of many kinds, because you know that the testing of your faith develops perseverance. Perseverance must finish its work so that you may be mature and complete, not lacking anything....

Blessed is the man who perseveres under trial, because when he has stood the test, he will receive the crown of life that God has promised to those who love him.

WHY DID GOD LET THIS HAPPEN?

The great Samuel Johnson once said about John Milton's *Paradise Lost* that although he knew many people who had 'read it,' he did not know many who had read it 'through'. That may be true of many literary classics. Books like Plato's *Republic*, Dante's *Divine Comedy*, Tolstoy's *War and Peace*, Melville's *Moby Dick*, and others are recognized as outstanding literary works. But there are millions of people who have never read them and have no intention of reading them.

The same is probably true of much biblical literature. In fact, even Christians probably neglect much of it. Many, I suppose, have never read 1 and 2 Chronicles or Jeremiah or Ezekiel or Lamentations. Or at least they have never read those biblical books 'through'.

When we talk about the New Testament one book that fits this category is James. Everybody knows about James. It is the book Martin Luther objected to. He said that it was not on the same level as the other biblical books, because it says so much about good works and not enough about faith. He called it 'a right strawy epistle'. We know *about* James. The problem is that although people know about James, many do not read it.

Why is this? In some cases it may be because of Luther's words; he rejected it, so we should reject it. I am convinced that for the most part James is neglected simply because it is so practical. James talks about wealth and how we use it, gossip, hypocrisy, how we choose our friends, and other such very practical things.

We find ourselves saying, 'I don't like that. Give me a good lecture on theology. Teach me about grace or justification. Better yet, let's discuss eschatology. Those subjects are interesting. But when you talk about who my friends should be, what I do with my mouth or with my disposable income, you are meddling where you shouldn't.'

Well, it is true. James does meddle in our most practical affairs, but in this he is only following the steps of his divine brother Jesus Christ, who did exactly that and was intensely practical. If we are to be Christ's disciples, we must hear and obey precisely this kind of instruction.

THE LORD'S BROTHER

Who was James? In the last paragraph I identified him as the Lord's brother, and I believe he is. But we should acknowledge that James does not specifically identify himself in this book, beyond merely using the name James in verse 1, and that there are a number of possible candidates for the book's author.

1. *James the son of Zebedee, the brother of John.* We know from the Book of Acts that this James was martyred, probably about AD 44. It would be nice to think of him as the author of this book, but most scholars believe that his death within fifteen years or so of the death and resurrection of Jesus eliminates this possibility. In their judgment the condition of the church described in James reflects a later period of church history.

2. *James the son of Alphaeus, also called James the less in contrast to the better-known James who was John's brother.* We know very little about this man, even though he was an apostle. He does not seem to have had a position of great leadership. Although his name, James, makes him a far-out possibility as author, there is no other reason to think of him as the writer of this letter.

3. *James the Lord's brother.* This man is mentioned in nine significant passages in the New Testament, apart from the Book of James. We know that he rose to importance in the early church, that he exercised leadership over the first church council described in Acts 15 (also see Gal. 2:1-10), and that he had a special ministry

to Jewish Christians, just as Paul and later Peter had special ministries to Gentiles. In view of this, it is hard not to think of this James as we come upon the opening words of the letter: 'James, a servant of God and of the Lord Jesus Christ, To the twelve tribes scattered among the nations: Greetings' (v. 1). This seems to be an apostle to the Jews writing to the Jews. And if this is the case, then James the Lord's brother is the most obvious candidate for being the book's author.

This would also explain why the teachings of James are so much like the Lord's teachings, as we will see they are, and why they are so practical. By some counts, there are twenty-two references to the Sermon on the Mount in this letter, and each of the Beatitudes is reflected in one way or another.

WHY DO THINGS GO WRONG?

As we might expect of a practical book by a practical man, James plunges at once into a practical problem. He introduces it as early as verse 2, saying, 'Consider it pure joy, my brothers, whenever you face trials of many kinds, because you know that the testing of your faith develops perseverance.' The problem James introduces is the problem we face when things do not go as we would like them to go or as we have planned them. It is the problem we have when we find ourselves asking, 'Why did this go wrong? Why did God let this happen? Why did this happen to me?'

Of all the questions I am asked, that is probably the one I have heard most often. Misfortunes come into our lives, unexplained tragedies occur, and we ask, 'Why? Why did this happen?'

James gives some practical examples. The first concerns a person who lacks worldly goods (v. 9), compared with a person who is rich (v. 10). James says, 'Don't take pride in either situation.' Reversals of fortune can happen overnight. Here is a person who through industry, commerce or the mere outworking of circumstances, has become relatively well off, and then suddenly he loses all he had. He is bound to ask, 'Why did this happen?' And 'Why did this happen to me rather than to someone else?'

Sometimes it is not a matter of wealth; it is a matter of position or prestige. We can go through a period of our lives where we are highly regarded. We are riding on a pinnacle of high public opinion. Then the winds of fortune change, and we are right back where we started. A person in these circumstances might well ask, 'Why?'

Pastors sometimes face these problems. I have a good friend who is in the Christian ministry and for nearly twenty years was used by God to start and then build up a solid evangelical church. It grew to more than one thousand members, had a strong missionary programme and exercised a valuable outreach to its affluent suburban community. But there were people in the church who were unhappy with the pastor. They didn't like his 'leadership style', as they put it. Suddenly he was asked to leave. It was a great and unexpected blow both to himself and his family. Why do such things happen? There was no immediate explanation.

Sometimes it is the loss of friends or family through death. Perhaps it is the death of a husband, a wife, a son or a daughter, or someone else important to our well-being, someone on whom we depended, someone to whom we looked for direction and understanding. Sometimes it is a person who seems essential to a certain work or ministry. When he or she is gone the ministry declines. When such a person is taken away, we find ourselves asking, 'Why? Why did this happen?'

There are two ways in which we can ask those questions. We can ask them with our fists clenched, shaking them at heaven in rebellion against God, saying to him, 'Why did you let this happen to me?' In that form the question is really an accusation. It means, 'If you are who you say you are, if you are a loving God, if you are true to your promises, none of these things should have happened.'

Or we can ask, as saints have asked down through the history of the Christian church when they found themselves in dreadful circumstances, 'Dear God, why is this happening? I am puzzled by it. Please explain it to me.' If you ask the question that way, if you are saying to God, 'I don't understand what is happening, because I live in a world where my horizons are limited and where, because of my sin, I certainly do not see things as you see them; I come to you for the insight you alone can provide,' then God, who is faithful to his people, may indeed provide some answers.

Some of these answers are given in the first chapter of James.

SOME REASONS WHY

There are four ways we can look at suffering.

1. *Some suffering is simply common to humanity.* Poetically, Job said, 'Man is born to trouble as surely as sparks fly upward' (Job 5:7). The word 'sparks' in our English Bibles actually translates two Hebrew words which mean 'sons of flame'. It is as though there is a great bonfire, and each generation is thrown upon the ashes of the generation that went before it. In time it too burns up and is gone.

Job is not saying that this is directly related to specific sin or shortcomings. It was not in his case. Job's sufferings were not related to any sinful thing he had done or even thought of doing. Job was saying that it is simply the common lot of men and women that we are born in pain, cause pain, endure pain and eventually die, often in pain.

This does not mean that God does not bring about his own purposes even in the suffering, but it does mean that we must not make the mistake the disciples made in Christ's day when they saw the man who had been born blind and immediately wanted to link his suffering to some specific sin either in him or his parents (cf. John 9:2). They were thinking, 'Sin produces suffering. There is a one-to-one relationship; therefore, it is either this man or his parents who are guilty.' But it is simply not true that when anyone is passing through a particularly difficult time this can always be linked to something sinful he or she has done. Therefore, Jesus answered, 'Neither this man nor his parents sinned, ... but this happened so that the work of God might be displayed in his life' (v. 3). In other words, in this man's case, suffering was an honour rather than a judgment.

2. *There is some suffering which we bring upon ourselves.* When James wrote about the rich man who lost his wealth, he was not implying that the rich man had been dishonest or had fleeced the poor to get his riches, or anything like that. However, it is possible to conceive of the case of a person who has lost his riches by over-extending himself through greed. It would be a case where he said, 'I am not satisfied with what I have. I want to have more. I want to invest in risky ventures, because I'm never really going to get to the top of the financial heap unless I do. I am going to take financial risks.' Then, as he takes chances, he loses everything he has. In such a case the loss of the riches would have been something that he had brought upon himself.

A person who dies of lung cancer after twenty or more years of smoking cigarettes cannot blame God for his cancer. He has brought it on himself. It is the same with problems caused by overeating, excessive drinking, taking harmful drugs, promiscuous sex, lying, giving vent to an unbridled temper, and many other such things. The suffering that comes from them is no one's fault but our own.

James may be thinking along these lines in verse 13, saying that certain things in us may bring misfortune. The example he gives is temptation to be greedy. 'When tempted, no one should say, "God is tempting me."' For God cannot be tempted by evil, nor does he tempt anyone; but each one is tempted when, by his own evil desire, he is dragged away and enticed. Then, after desire has conceived, it gives birth to sin; and sin, when it is full-grown, gives birth to death' (vv. 13-15). He is saying that sometimes the things we go through are the product of our own sinful choices.

3. *Some suffering is intended by God for our good, to develop our character and make us like Jesus Christ.* God brings certain problems into our lives in order to perfect us, mould us or shape us into the kind of men and women he would have us be. 'Consider it pure joy, my brothers, whenever you face trials of many kinds, because you know that the testing of your faith develops perseverance. Perseverance must finish its work so that you may be mature and complete, not lacking anything' (vv. 2-4).

If you want to develop a strong physical body, you have to do it by strenuous exercise. Sitting around and simply enjoying yourself, eating candy and roasted marshmallows, will never produce an athlete. If you want to be strong and have a well-developed body, you must get out on the track. You have to begin with jogging. You have to do your exercises. You have to endure hardship in order to tone up your muscles.

So also with character. The person who has never gone through any struggle, who has never had any misfortune in his or her life, who has never suffered any kind of loss, will not develop the kind of character that can endure calamity. And certainly such a person will not have the kind of character that will be able to instruct and help other people. James says that some misfortune is sent, not because of sin or even because it is the common lot of humanity, but simply because God wants it to develop traits of strong Christian character that would not be developed in any other way.

Perseverance with patience is one of those traits. Sometimes a person comes to his minister and says, 'I am a poor specimen of

Christianity. I have no patience at all. Would you please pray for me that I might have patience?' A minister who knows the Word of God well might begin to pray at that moment, 'Lord, please send tribulation into this person's life,' because the way we develop perseverance of patience is through suffering. Therefore, if misfortune enters your life, God may be using it to develop character in you that in days to come he will use to bring glory to his name.

4. *Some suffering is to bring God glory.* The fourth purpose in misfortune is that by it God might be glorified. That is, the suffering is not merely the common lot of man, nor is it something we bring upon ourselves by our sin or misconduct, nor is it sent by God in order to develop our Christian character. It is to glorify the name of God only. We have already alluded to two cases in which this was the reason for an individual's great suffering.

The first case is that of the man born blind, found in John 9. I mentioned it briefly above because of the disciples' question: 'Rabbi, who sinned, this man or his parents, that he was born blind?' (v. 2). They were assuming that suffering is always the result of a prior sin – this is a moral universe, after all – but they were broad-minded enough to acknowledge that the sin that caused the blindness might not have been that of the man himself but might rather have been the sin of his parents.

That was a possible explanation, of course. We do not know if they understood anything about the transmission of disease, but we know that blindness in children can be caused by venereal disease in the parents. So it could be the case that his suffering was because of their sin. How he could have been born blind because of his own sin is a bit more problematic, unless they were thinking of his sin in a previous life and were therefore assuming the doctrine of reincarnation.

In any case, Jesus stated that neither was the cause. He said, 'Neither this man nor his parents sinned, but this happened so that the work of God might be displayed in his life' (v. 3). In other words, Jesus said that the man was born blind so that at this particular moment Jesus might come along and heal him and thus bring God glory.

A life time of blindness just so God might be glorified? Yes! That is what Jesus said. Not all suffering is like this, of course – I have been pointing out other reasons for it – but some is, and this was a particularly dramatic case. Of course, Jesus also led this man to faith in himself so that the display of the glory of God in the blind man's circumstances also, and primarily, resulted in his being saved from sin and entering into eternal life. His passing from blindness to sight symbolized his passing from spiritual darkness to spiritual light and was the setting for Jesus' powerful saying, 'I am the light of the world' (v. 5).

The Pharisees, who are the protagonists in the story, did not see this, did not believe on Jesus and so remained in darkness.

The second case is Job, who is probably an even clearer illustration of a righteous person suffering solely that God might be glorified. We are going to be looking at Job's story in detail later on, because he is mentioned by James specifically in chapter 5, verse 11. But it is worth noting here that the point of the story is that Job had not done anything to deserve what he was going through. His friends thought he had. They argued, 'No one has ever suffered quite as much as you are suffering, Job. We are sorry for you. But remember, God does not run a universe in which there is no correspondence between suffering and sin. So if you are suffering a lot, it is because you have sinned. Furthermore, because you are suffering a lot, you must have sinned a lot. What you need to do is come clean, confess it. Then, perhaps God will straighten things out again.'

The problem with that argument was that Job knew his heart. He did not suppose he was sinless. No godly man would think that. But he knew that he had not done anything so dreadfully bad that God was punishing him. Job wrestles with this question throughout the entire book.

What was God's purpose? We find it at the beginning where God calls Satan's attention to Job as an upright godly man. Satan retorted that Job served God only because God had made him rich and later that he served God only because he was afraid that he might lose his health. God denied this and determined to put the devil's slander to the test by allowing Satan to take away Job's possessions and health. Satan did. But at the end, Job did not curse God, as Satan had predicted. Job blessed God instead. Thus, God was glorified by Job and the ways of God were vindicated.

JOB'S SUFFERING AND OURS

What does this have to say about our sufferings? It says that, although suffering sometimes comes to us because of our sin and sometimes as God's way of developing Christian character in us, it also sometimes is God's way of bringing glory to his own name – something that is possible only through the suffering of his people.

You ask, 'But how can I know why I am suffering? You've talked about the possibilities, but when I'm going through it, how can I know what's happening?'

Well, you can't always know. As far as we can tell, Job never fully understood what had happened to him.

But that is not the whole answer. For James says, 'If any of you lacks wisdom, he should ask God, who gives generously to all without finding fault, and it will be given to him' (v. 5). Ask God to show you what he is doing.

God may not give the answer right away, of course. Or at all.

WHY DID GOD LET THIS HAPPEN?

But if God does not give the answer, there is still something we can know, something James mentions in verses 17 and 18: 'Every good and perfect gift is from above, coming down from the Father of the heavenly lights, who does not change like shifting shadows. He chose to give us birth through the word of truth, that we might be a kind of firstfruits of all he created.' In other words, while waiting for God's answer, we can at least know that God loves us and that we are among the firstfruits of his important new creation, regardless of what we may be suffering.

2

I DON'T WANT
TO BE A FANATIC
(James 1:19-27)

Do not merely listen to the word, and so deceive yourselves. Do what it says. Anyone who listens to the word but does not do what it says is like a man who looks at his face in a mirror and, after looking at himself, goes away and immediately forgets what he looks like. But the man who looks intently into the perfect law that gives freedom, and continues to do this, not forgetting what he has heard, but doing it – he will be blessed in what he does.

I DON'T WANT TO BE A FANATIC

Have you ever thought that it is acceptable to be a fanatic about almost anything but religion?

Everyone accepts the sports fanatic. The word 'fan' is derived from fanatic; so a sports fanatic is merely a fanatic for his team. I know joggers whom I would call fanatics. No matter what the weather is, they are outside jogging. The motto of the United States postal service is the well-known classical quotation: 'Neither rain nor snow, nor sleet nor hail, nor gloom of night, shall stay these brave couriers from the swift completion of their appointed rounds.' I think that applies to these joggers, which is why I think of them as fanatics. Fanaticism is obviously acceptable in most areas of life. But when you talk about religion, the subject of utmost and ultimate importance, people fear fanaticism. They do not mind toying with religious ideas, but they do not want to become committed to them. They say, 'I don't want to be fanatical about it.'

James is talking about that kind of attitude when he says, 'Do not merely listen to the word, and so deceive yourselves. Do what it says' (Jas. 1:22). A person who really does what it says is fanatical about it.

A 'HOLY SPIRIT FAN'

Though it may not be acceptable to be a religious fanatic these days, it is only in religion that the word 'fanatic' may actually be properly used. This is because 'fanatic' is derived from the Latin word *fanaticus*, which means 'to be inspired by divinity'. A fanatical person was one upon whom the spirit of a god had come. In the Christian sense, then, a fanatic would be one upon whom the Holy Spirit has come to lead him or her to a knowledge of the truth about God and to a life style in accordance with that truth.

The Epistle of James is difficult to outline. Someone has likened it to a series of sermon notes. Or it might also be compared to a string of beads. Each item is important, but it is not always easy to determine why each bead is placed where it is. However, in this section, in which James discusses being committed to what one professes, the sequence of thought does seem clear. The first half of the chapter has treated testing and temptation. But, as James wrote, he must have realized that some of his readers might say, 'If that is the kind of religion you're talking about, a religion in which patience is to be achieved only by trials, suffering, hardship and tribulation, I'm not sure I really want to commit myself to it.'

James could have pointed out Old Testament examples of those who achieved patience through suffering, but if he had, he would only have made matters worse. Any list of Old Testament examples would certainly include Job, whose story we looked at in the last chapter. Job had been abundantly blessed by God in terms of this world's goods. He also had a godly family, seven sons and three daughters all serving the Lord. In addition, he was in good health. Then suddenly, all in a day, this was taken away. And the whole point of the story is that this was not because of any special sin in Job. God allowed it to happen simply to show that a man or woman will worship and serve God not for what God gives but because of who God is. This was something Satan did not understand. But God showed it before Satan, the fallen and unfallen angels, and to us also through Scripture.

Although it is true that at the end God restored Job's blessing, a person might well object, 'If that is what it means to be truly committed to God, I'm not sure I want any of it. I don't want to be that fanatical.'

Or again, we could consider Abraham. He is a great example of testing. Abraham began with what we would regard as a rudimentary faith. God appeared to him in a vision and said, 'Abraham, I want you to leave your homeland and go to a land that I am going to show you. I am going to bless you and make your name great. I will multiply your descendants, and you will become a source of blessing not merely to these, your own people, but also to all the nations of the world.'

Abraham started out. At the beginning, he did not have a great deal of faith, but God began to work in his life in order to develop his faith further. At times there were famines, and Abraham did not know where he was going to get enough to eat. On another occasion marauders came out of the desert and carried off the produce, livestock and people of Sodom, including Abraham's nephew Lot. At great risk to himself, Abraham pursued and attacked the marauders and brought the goods and people back.

Finally there was a spiritual test. Abraham, who was now becoming strong in the faith, was told by God to take his son Isaac and sacrifice him on a distant mountain. This must have produced a great struggle within Abraham, but he obeyed God and climbed that mountain with his son. You will remember how dramatically God stopped him just as Abraham was on the verge of killing his son. Through that experience Abraham was taught something of what it would mean for God himself to give his only-begotten Son on the cross for our salvation. Abraham learned these lessons through the things he suffered.

But a person might not think that very valuable, or at least not worth the cost of learning it. Such a person might respond, 'If that is what it means to be Christian, I'm not sure I want to go along with it.'

The examples of Job and Abraham are certainly extreme cases. Not many are called to undergo testing like that. But to be honest, it is probably not the examples of Job and Abraham that bother us as much as it is the very kind of things that James talks about in these verses. As he begins to talk about 'doing the word', what James mentions specifically is not great feats of heroism, but simply matters like controlling our speech, being slow to anger, caring for orphans and widows, and personal righteousness. This is the theme of the verses.

Look at them. 'My dear brothers, take note of this: Everyone should be quick to listen, slow to speak and slow to become angry, for man's anger does not bring about the righteous life that God desires. Therefore, get rid of all moral filth and the evil that is so prevalent, and humbly accept the word planted in you, which can save you.

'Do not merely listen to the word, and so deceive yourselves. Do what it says. Anyone who listens to the word but does not do what it says is like a man who looks at his face in a mirror and, after looking at himself, goes away and immediately forgets what he looks like. But the man who looks intently into the perfect law that gives freedom, and continues to do this, not forgetting what he has heard, but doing it – he will be blessed in what he does.

'If anyone considers himself religious and yet does not keep a tight rein on his tongue, he deceives himself and his religion is worthless. Religion that God our Father accepts as pure and faultless is this: to look after orphans and widows in their distress and to keep oneself from being polluted by the world' (Jas. 2:19-27).

'Is that fanaticism?' In the biblical sense, it is. Our problem comes not from our reluctance to be heroes and heroines, but from our reluctance to carry out the implications of the gospel in the tiny details of our personal conduct and lives – fanatically.

SOME PRACTICAL EXAMPLES

Think of the matters that James mentions.

1. *Control of our tongues.* James says more about speech than anyone else in Scripture, undoubtedly because he had seen the many bad effects of ill temper or loose speech. He speaks of words that lead to anger. He says, 'Don't let that happen. Control

it. Be slow to speak, because anger does not produce the kind of righteousness that God desires.'

In the last chapter I mentioned that James refers often to the Sermon on the Mount. We have an example here. You will remember that Jesus also regarded anger as a serious matter, noting that anger cannot be lightly excused by saying, 'Well, it's true I lost control a little bit. But I've always had a bad temper. My father had a bad temper too, and I just inherited it. It runs in the family.' Jesus did not dismiss anger that easily. He said that anger and the speech that results from it are like murder. As he did in all his ethical teaching, he put his finger on the thoughts and intents of the heart, showing what ultimately flows from these if evil thoughts and anger go unchecked.

He said, 'Some of you say *raca* to your brother.' (Raca was a term of contempt.) 'Some of you call other people fools.' (The word he used is *moros*, which means one who is a moral fool, an unscrupulous, unethical person; it is a slander on his conduct.) Jesus said, 'Anyone who says, "You fool!" will be in danger of the fire of hell' (Matt. 5:22; see v. 21).

Here James says that one who is committed to Jesus Christ should have his tongue under strict control.

2. *Personal righteousness.* I do not know whether James was thinking of the Sermon on the Mount specifically at this point, but, if he was, he was probably thinking of our Lord's words: 'Be perfect, therefore, as your heavenly Father is perfect' (Matt. 5:48). James describes the righteous life God desires as getting rid 'of all moral filth and the evil that is so prevalent' in our age (Jas. 1:21).

We live in an age characterized by moral filth, even as James did. The danger of contamination by the world through its entertainment, magazines, books and even day-to-day living, is something we know very well. James is telling us to keep ourselves free from all that and not to be contaminated by such things.

Recently a businessman said to me, 'It is unbelievable, the kind of things that go on in the financial world.'

I asked, 'What do you mean? Do you mean that people manipulate the books?'

He replied, 'Worse than that. People are downright dishonest even with their clients.'

I said, 'You mean they rob from the rich in order also to rob from the poor?'

He said, 'You've got it exactly.'

James says that we are to keep ourselves free from such things if we are followers of Jesus Christ.

3. *Care of the unfortunate.* In verse 27 James says that religion that is 'pure and faultless is this: to look after orphans and widows in their distress and to keep oneself from being polluted by the world.'

Why is it that we think we can neglect acts of social righteousness? Earlier in this century American evangelicalism was characterized by this wrong attitude. Perhaps it was because evangelicals were so concerned about the gospel or about the doctrine of justification by grace through faith that they did not want anything to detract from it. They did not want to stress good works at all. Maybe that was the reason. I do not know. Perhaps there were other reasons. All I know is that for a long time American evangelicals were deficient in this area.

Isn't it amazing that, when writing about the essence of pure religion, James can focus not on a doctrinal matter, but on a matter of righteous, personal conduct? Of course, he is not talking about the *content* of faith. If he had said that the essence of the content of the Christian faith is to take care of widows and orphans, he would have been wrong. The content of the Christian faith is the atoning death and victorious resurrection of Jesus Christ. Care of orphans, widows and other acts of charity, is not the content of Christianity but the expression of it. As I said, the content of the gospel is God's work through Christ for our salvation.

But let me approach this another way. Note that James is writing about 'religion', saying that the practical expression of one's religion is caring for others. Religion is the practice of one's faith. The word 'religion' is composed of two Latin words: *re*, which means 'again', and *ligeo*, which means 'to bind together'. We get our word 'ligament' from it. So religion is 'that which binds things together again'. In other words, it is faith at work, faith practicing. Religion is faith beginning to make things work together properly again, as they should work.

WHY BE PRACTICAL?

These are the matters about which James wants us to be fanatical. He wants us to be fanatical in controlling our tongues, fanatical where our own personal morality is concerned, and fanatical in caring for other people.

You say, 'I'm not sure I want to do it. It sounds too difficult. Why should I be concerned about this?'

Let me give you the answers James has in these verses.

I. *Self-knowledge.* It is only by practicing what we hear that we come to know ourselves. In other words, self-knowledge is wrapped up with the faithful practice of religion. This is what he is talking about by his image of the mirror. The mirror is Scripture, of course. When you look into the Word, like a mirror, and see what it says, the teaching you discover should cause you to understand yourself and your shortcomings, and thus lead you to apply yourself to the law of God so you might live differently.

What person takes a mirror, glances in it and then looks away and does nothing at all? You look into a mirror to see if something needs to be done about your appearance. Have you washed your face? Have you combed your hair? Is your dress properly ironed? Is your tie on straight? You look in the mirror to see things as they are.

James says that when you read about true Christianity and see the kind of life that you are to live, it is not so you can go out and speak learnedly about that kind of life. It is so you can go out and live that life yourself. So the first thing that happens when you look carefully into the requirements of Christianity, as you find them in the Bible, is that you find out what kind of person you are. Are you really doing those things? Or are you only pretending to do them? Are you doing some of those things but not others? Are you doing the superficial things but not the important things? The only place you will find answers to those questions is in the Word of God. The only place you ever really find out about yourself is in the Bible.

We all have very distorted ideas of ourselves. Your spouse may know what you are like, but the person who probably knows least what you are really like is yourself.

In *How to Win Friends and Influence People*, the well-known motivational speaker Dale Carnegie tells the story of a New York gangster known as 'Two-Gun' Crowley, who was well known in the early decades of this century. On one occasion a policeman stopped his car and asked to see his licence. Crowley reached into his vest pocket, pulled out one of the two guns he always carried, and shot the policeman. Then he took the policeman's own gun and shot him again. That was the kind of man he was, cruel and violent. He became the subject of an intensive manhunt, and eventually the place where he was hiding was surrounded by the police and Crowley was captured.

What did Crowley think about himself? Did he say, 'I'm a bad man; I shoot policemen'? Not at all. After he was captured, the police found a note in his girl friend's apartment, where he had been during the shoot-out. It was bloodstained as a result of the battle. On this note he had scribbled the words: 'Underneath this coat beats a warm heart, a kind one, one that would do nobody any harm.' When they finally took him to Sing-Sing prison and executed him, his last words were: 'This is what I get for defending myself.'

If a hoodlum like 'Two-Gun' Crowley does not see the evil in his life, it is certain that you and I, the supposedly 'good people', do not see it unless God reveals it to us through his Word. I say again that the only way we can find out what we are like is if we come face to face with the things the Lord Jesus Christ commands us to do if we are serious about living for him in this world.

2. *Acceptance with God.* In addition to learning about ourselves, we also find what we must do to please God. This is what James says in verse 27: 'Religion that God our Father accepts as pure and faultless is this: to look after orphans and widows in their distress and to keep oneself from being polluted by the world.'

The word 'accept' is used in different ways in the Bible. There is an acceptance of us by God in Christ which has to do with our justification. When Paul writes in Ephesians 1:6 that God has made us 'accepted in the Beloved' (KJV), he is referring to this kind of acceptance. This is not what James has in mind, however. James is thinking more along the lines that Paul was when he wrote in Philippians 4:18, speaking of the service of the saints in Philippi as an 'acceptable sacrifice'. What they did was acceptable to God, because it was in accordance with what he laid out for them to do in Scripture.

When James says, 'Religion that God our Father accepts ... is this,' he is implying that there is a religion that is not acceptable to God. What is it? Obviously, unacceptable religion is a religion of words only, a faith unmatched by good deeds.

3. *Personal blessing.* This truly religious life, in addition to giving us self-knowledge and acceptance with God, provides us with personal blessing. In verse 25 James says, 'The man who looks intently into the perfect law that gives freedom, and continues to do this, not forgetting what he has heard, but doing it – he will be blessed in what he does.'

I ask the question, 'Do you want God to bless you?'

'Of course, I do,' you answer.

Well, then, here is how to get it: 1) read the Bible, 2) find out what it says, and 3) live by what you find there. Simple? Yes. But how many actually do it?

4. *Blessing for other people.* Finally, not only does this conduct provide blessing for us, it provides blessing for other people as well. Can we imagine that where we are quick to listen, slow to speak, and slow to anger, blessing will not come to people with whom we would otherwise be angry and slow to listen to? When we read that we are to keep ourselves from the moral filth and evil so prevalent in the world, are we to think that could ever be without blessing in the lives of those with whom we have contact? When we look after the orphans, widows, and others in need of special attention, can we think that such behavior will not be a blessing to them? Of course not. In all these things other people are blessed through our obedience. Thus, when we do these things, we become something of what the Lord Jesus Christ obviously desired for his disciples when he said, 'You are the salt of the earth' (Matt. 5:13) and 'the light of the world' (v. 14).

There are all kinds of fanatics. Some are very quiet fanatics. I know of one young woman from a Jewish background who went home for a bar-mitzvah. Her sister pleaded with her, 'When you come home, please do not spoil this bar-mitzvah.' What she meant was, 'Don't talk about Jesus.' This woman asked for prayer, saying, 'I have no desire to spoil anything that goes on, but what am I to answer when they remark, "Oh, I haven't seen you for such a long time. What's new?"' She had only one answer: 'What's new is Jesus.' I think I would call that woman a fanatic, and I would desire that we might all be fanatics in that sense.

The message of James is that we should all become fanatics not only by our presentation of the gospel, but also by our day-to-day conduct. Then we will find that others will want to become fans of Jesus too.

3

MY FRIENDS ARE SPECIAL
(James 2:1-13)

My brothers, as believers in our glorious Lord Jesus Christ, don't show favoritism. Suppose a man comes into your meeting wearing a gold ring and fine clothes, and a poor man in shabby clothes also comes in. If you show special attention to the man wearing fine clothes and say, 'Here's a good seat for you,' but say to the poor man, 'You stand there' or 'Sit on the floor by my feet,' have you not discriminated among yourselves and become judges with evil thoughts?

Choosing friends is something you usually want to do for yourself.

If you do not believe that, ask a teenager. It seems that nothing is so important to teenagers as their friends. If you want to lose your teenage children, drive their friends away. You will soon find your children going away with them. On the other hand, if you can draw their friends in and include them as part of your family, you will find that your children will stay with you too.

The value of friendships may be seen most vividly among teenagers, but the same tendency is apparent in adults, isn't it? We want to be able to choose our own friends, and we do not want others to tell us whom we should or should not like.

Unfortunately, this can come into conflict with our Christian walk, if we choose friends for the wrong reasons.

In a little essay called *The Inner Ring*, C. S. Lewis analyzed our desires to make friends of the right people. He noted that whenever we are part of a group, we are concerned not merely to be part of the group but to get to the inner circle of that group, to get close to the people who seem to provide the group's inner dynamic or the leadership for it. Yet when we succeed in that, we soon discover that there is a circle within the circle. We try to enter that, then the circle after that. Lewis argued that this is a hopeless endeavor, because no matter which circles you enter, there are always other circles that seem more desirable, and beyond them others which are even more exclusive.

Lewis contrasted that wrong desire with the attitude of God, who did not set up little exclusive circles but reached out beyond the truly 'inner' circle of the Godhead to include people who otherwise would have had no hope of being included. God extended his grace to us in the Lord Jesus Christ, thereby reaching out to bring us into fellowship with himself.

RICH MAN, POOR MAN

This is the problem James discusses in the first half of the second chapter of his epistle: favoritism or exclusiveness. In these verses, James describes the problem of exclusiveness in such pointed and specific language that we are convinced he is describing what he himself had seen in the church at Jerusalem, where he was working.

'My brothers, as believers in our glorious Lord Jesus Christ, don't show favoritism. Suppose a man comes into your meeting wearing a gold ring and fine clothes, and a poor man in shabby clothes also comes in. If you show special attention to the man wearing fine clothes and say, 'Here's a good seat for you,' but say to the poor man, 'You stand there' or 'Sit on the floor by my feet,' have you not discriminated among yourselves and become judges with evil thoughts?' (vv. 1-4).

But it was not just in Jerusalem that this problem existed. We see it around us in our own circles too.

Frank E. Gaebelein, a former headmaster of the Stony Brook School on Long Island, wrote a short but wise exposition of James. He asked, 'Have we not seen the same thing in our churches today? The human heart does not change; we of this twentieth century have also held the faith of our Lord Jesus Christ, the Lord of glory, in respect of persons. Thinking of the rich as potential sources of money for our work, we have sometimes lavished upon them undeserved attention and flattery, while treating the poor with scant courtesy. The plain fact is that such actions, whenever found in the Christian church, reveal deplorable lack of faith. Were we looking wholly to God for help, we should not be making these distinctions. It must also be admitted that few things in the New Testament are more disregarded in Christian work than this principle of not respecting persons. We can only accept the rebuke, saying with new determination to trust God more completely: "Brethren, these things ought not so to be."' [1]

We tend to give preference to the people the world judges important, don't we? People who have money, power or position get special attention.

It is even the case that in our day some of our approaches to evangelism promote this openly. They focus on the important people, arguing that if they reach the important people, the rest will follow along, moved by their example. That does not follow, of course. No one is born again by the mere example of another. Regeneration is a work of God, and God does not show favoritism. On the contrary, 'God chose the foolish things of the world to shame the wise; God chose the weak things of the world to shame the strong. He chose the lowly things of this world and the despised things – and the things that are not – to nullify the things that are, so that no one may boast before him' (1 Cor. 1:27-29).

This must mean that an approach to evangelism that deliberately focuses on the 'important' people exclusively is wrong.

But we also need to say that the opposite is just as wrong. Some people take this approach, arguing that the gospel is for the poor, first of all. And because they emphasize this so much, they almost end up saying that the gospel is for the poor only. They find themselves thinking that the rich or important people somehow don't deserve it. They say, 'I'm not going to have anything to do with those rich people. They persecute the poor. They are the cause of the problem.' That approach can be equally bad.

And here is another qualification.

We should not even say that an evangelistic strategy that emphasizes a particular stratum of society is necessarily non-Christian. It all depends on what you are trying to do. If you are

---

1. Frank E. Gaebelein, *The Practical Epistle of James: Studies in Applied Christianity* (Great Neck, NY; Channel Press, 1955), p. 59.

working in a high school and are trying to reach a broad spectrum of the high school students, it may be wise to try to reach the natural leaders of the age group first, because teenagers are very peer-oriented. In that way the evangelist may have greater opportunity to reach the others. He is reaching the first group because he is concerned about the others and very much wants to reach them too.

On the other hand, there is unfortunately a kind of evangelism that seeks to reach the important people – athletic stars, Hollywood personalities or political celebrities – simply to parade them before audiences as trophies. And this, as I have already suggested, is as wrong as it is offensive. There should be no place for it among true Christians.

CONFRONTING THE PROBLEM
But enough of the problem. What we need to see is how James dealt with what he saw happening in the church at Jerusalem, because what he says can be a pattern for how we can deal with the same wrongful discrimination between the supposedly 'important' and the supposedly 'unimportant' people in our churches today. Or in our own conduct.

1. *The example of Jesus Christ.* In verses 1-4, James points his readers to the pattern of the Lord Jesus Christ. I mean by this that it is no accident that, as James begins this chapter, he says, 'My brothers, *as believers in our glorious Lord Jesus Christ*, don't show favoritism.' His emphasis is on Jesus Christ, and the reason for it is to remind his readers of Jesus' strong example.

The word 'glorious' is important too. By referring to Jesus Christ as 'glorious', James is reminding us not of the lowly, poor Jesus of the days of his earthly humiliation, but of the Jesus who existed in glory with the Father before the incarnation and who exists in that same glory now. This is the Christ who for our sakes, as Paul says in Philippians 2, divested himself of his outward glory and became obedient to death for our sakes.

> Who, being in very nature God,
>   did not consider equality with God something to be grasped,
> but made himself nothing,
>   taking the very nature of a servant,
>   being made in human likeness.
> And being found in appearance as a man,
>   he humbled himself
>   and became obedient to death –
>   even death on a cross!   (vv. 6-8).

James is saying, 'If, in your dealings within the Christian assembly, you are showing special attention to those who are thought to be important, be challenged by the example of our Lord. He *was* important. He was and is the Lord of glory. But if he had acted on the basis of who was important, either himself or others, he certainly would never have come to earth to die for us. What he did do was lay his glorious prerogatives aside so that he might identify with and save people like you and me, people with no earthly importance whatever.'

Perhaps James also mentions Jesus Christ as an example of a desirable life style. Who is the Jesus we know? The Jesus we know is the Christ of the Gospels, the one who went about as a poor man in the midst of a poor, oppressed people, doing good, teaching them and dying for their salvation. This is the one we have come to know and love.

Therefore, when James mentions Christ, he is directing our thoughts to him so we might gain a proper perspective and have a sound example.

2. *The value of the individual.* In verses 5 through 7, James speaks about the inherent value of the person who is poor and therefore often unimportant in the world's eyes. It is true that God also saves rich people, but in the Bible he seems to express a special concern for the poor. In his book *Rich Christians in an Age of Hunger,* Ronald J. Sider points out the acute physical need of vast numbers of people in our world. Then, quoting repeatedly from the Old Testament as well as from the New, he demonstrates the great concern that God has for poor people.

This does not mean that God is not concerned for those who are better off also, of course. If God were concerned only for the poor, not many in the western world would be saved, because in comparison with the poor of this world, most of us are very well off indeed. It does mean, however, that God has a special concern for those who are deprived of this world's goods, those who are poor in material things. Indeed, the Bible suggests that God has worked so that these, though poor in this world's goods, might become rich in faith and other spiritual resources.

The question James is asking is something like this: If God has acted in this way, if God has reached out to save the poor whom he counts as of special value, should not that also be the stance and attitude of those who are his people?

3. *The conduct of those who are favored.* With what seems to be an ironic twist, James next reminds his readers that those rich people to whom they give such deference have not always treated them very well. 'Is it not the rich who are exploiting you? Are they not the ones who are dragging you into court? Are they not the ones who are slandering the noble name of him to whom you belong?' (vv. 6, 7). That is a sobering set of questions which in turn suggests some sober reflection. Is it not true that the problems of God's people come mostly from those who are rich, influential

or are thought to be important?

This was obviously very true in the early days of the church. The book of Acts gives many examples of the important people's treatment of those who were judged poor or unimportant.

In Acts 4 we read of the imprisonment of Peter and John by 'the priests and the captain of the temple guard and the Sadducees,' that is, by those who were the privileged class or the upper crust of their day (v. 1). This was the first formal opposition to the early preachers, to the gospel and to the church, and it came from the important people. They were opposed to the early preaching because it made them look bad and was perceived as a threat to their privileged position in Jerusalem.

In Acts 13, when Paul and Barnabas were in Antioch of Pisidia, the two missionaries were persecuted by the 'women of high standing and the leading men of the city,' probably because they were the people who had most to lose if there was any trouble in the city. Those who have high standing can be quite ruthless in opposing anyone who threatens their position. They were then. They are today also.

In Acts 19, as the result of Paul's preaching in Ephesus, some of the business of those who had been producing idols of Artemis (Diana) of the Ephesians had begun to fall off, and they were in an uproar. Didn't they believe in freedom of religion? Of course! Freedom of religion is usually affirmed so long as people's business is not affected by it. But when business is affected there is trouble, and that was the case here. Those who had something to lose stirred up the Ephesian people, causing a riot, and Paul eventually had to leave the city.

'So,' James asks, 'why are you paying special attention to people like that? Aren't you aware that those are the very people who have made life so difficult for your brothers, not only here in Jerusalem but in other places in the world?'

This argument may not affect most of us in exactly the same way as James intended it to affect the Christians of his day. Conditions today are probably somewhat different, at least on the surface. But James' argument should open our minds to what God is doing among the underprivileged in our day and should even challenge us to work among them in order that many might come to faith in Jesus Christ. Is it not true that in the perspective of the Lord we are all poor, we are all underprivileged, we are all nobodies who only by his grace may become somebodies by responding to the gospel? That is exactly what we are. So we of all people ought to reach out to those who have no stature in this world's eyes so that, as the gospel is preached to them and they respond to it, they might find their true stature before God.

DEALING WITH SIN

Throughout this section of the chapter James' argument builds in force and intensity. He has alluded to Jesus Christ and his example (v. 1). He has talked about God's estimate of the poor as opposed to the way most people think of them (v. 5). Next he has reminded us that the oppression of the poor is caused, more often than not, by the rich (vv. 6, 7). Now, beginning with verse 8, he speaks even more forcefully, saying that the favoritism we practice but think of as unimportant is actually a very serious sin. It is a sin that will bring us into judgment.

'If you really keep the royal law found in Scripture, "Love your neighbor as yourself," you are doing right. But if you show favoritism, you sin and are convicted by the law [that is, by that law, the law of Leviticus 19:18] as lawbreakers. For whoever keeps the whole law and yet stumbles at just one point is guilty of breaking all of it. For he who said, "Do not commit adultery," also said, "Do not murder." If you do not commit adultery but do commit murder, you have become a lawbreaker' (vv. 8-11).

James is quoting 'Love your neighbor as yourself' from Leviticus 19:18, as I indicated. But perhaps he is also thinking of the teaching of Jesus as recorded in Matthew 22. Jesus had been asked about the greatest commandment, and he had responded by summarizing the law in two parts. First, 'Love the Lord your God with all your heart and with all your soul and with all your mind.' Second, 'Love your neighbor as yourself.' Jesus said, 'All the Law and the Prophets hang on these two commandments' (vv. 37-40).

What James adds is that, if you break that law – and you do break it if you show favoritism, because you are not loving that neighbor as yourself – then you have broken not only that law and stand condemned by it, but you have also broken the entire law as well.

What should you do when you sin? Christians know the answer to that. First, you should confess it as sin before God. Second, you should ask God's forgiveness. Third, you should turn your back on the sin and determine to go in a different way entirely. As far as favoritism goes, this means that you should begin to behave as well or better toward the disadvantaged of this world as you have been behaving toward those you think are important.

JUDGMENT AND MERCY

At the end of this section James speaks of mercy and judgment: 'Speak and act as those who are going to be judged by the law that gives freedom, because judgment without mercy will be shown to anyone who has not been merciful. Mercy triumphs over judgment!' (vv. 12, 13).

In these verses he reminds us that there is such a thing as judgment and that judgment will fall on those who break God's law. In the light of the coming judgment James urges us to re-examine our relationships with other people as well as with God. Of course, James is not teaching salvation by works. He is not saying that if you keep this law and the next law and the law after that, you will be saved by keeping the law. What he is teaching is this: If you are showing favoritism, consider carefully what you are doing, because you are breaking God's law, and stop doing it. Knowing what you are doing should cause you to re-examine your relationship to God and start to behave differently. And you will behave differently if you are a Christian!

If you are related to God the Father, as you should be in Jesus Christ, something of the spirit of Christ that went out to those who were destitute, needy, poor and unimportant should be in you, and you should find yourself showing mercy to them even as Jesus did. This is how Christians must behave and operate. Therefore, if you are not doing this, you should re-examine yourself to see if you are really saved.

Sometimes people have read James' letter and said, 'There is no gospel in James.' Martin Luther is one who did this, which is why he called it 'a right strawy epistle'. But it is not true that there is no gospel in James. True, James is a practical book. James is not writing, as Paul did in Romans or one of his other epistles, to expose our sin and explain God's answer to that sin through the death of Christ. But the gospel is in James all the same. James has already spoken of our need to be born again in the first chapter, and in the beginning of this chapter he has spoken of our need for faith in Christ. Now he adds to this that, if we are believers, each of us must be living a life which matches our profession.

That is really the bottom line. We read the Word; we know the teaching; we can give discourses on what the doctrine says. But James asks, 'Does your life match the things you teach and, in particular, does it match up in this very important matter of choosing who are to be your friends?'

Who are your friends? They should be those who are friendless, those who do not attract the attention of the world, those who would be neglected if it were not for Christian people. Jesus reached out to such people. You also should reach out to them and include them for the sake of the Lord Jesus Christ and the Gospel.

4

SURE, I BELIEVE, SO WHAT?
(James 2:14-26)

What good is it, my brothers, if a man claims to have faith but has no deeds? Can such a faith save him? Suppose a brother or sister is without clothes and daily food. If one of you says to him, 'Go, I wish you well; keep warm and well fed,' but does nothing about his physical needs, what good is it? In the same way, faith by itself, if it is not accompanied by action, is dead.

But someone will say, 'You have faith; I have deeds.'

Show me your faith without deeds, and I will show you my faith by what I do. You believe that there is one God. Good! Even the demons believe that – and shudder.

In his epistles, especially Romans, Galatians and Ephesians, the apostle Paul stressed that we are saved by grace through faith, not by works. This teaching, salvation by faith apart from works, became the great doctrine of the Reformation at the time of Martin Luther. Protestants and many Catholics hold to it firmly today. Yet as we read the latter half of the second chapter of this epistle, James seems to be saying that we are saved by works, or at least by faith plus works. Furthermore, he is saying that if works are not present, we are lost.

Through the centuries people have read James and Paul and have had understandable problems with the apparent contradiction. No less a student of the Bible and a leader of the church than Martin Luther was troubled by it, and on the basis of this passage and its apparent teaching he developed a low regard for the entire epistle. He felt that James did not have the weight of the gospel in it. In the same way, because of this problem many people pass over the very practical teaching of the book.

This is unfortunate, of course. For the verses we are going to consider now deal with this matter of faith and works very practically, and what they say needs to be understood, believed and appropriated no less today than in the time of James. It is a matter we should carefully explore.

WORKS DO MATTER

Basically, the issue hinges on the notion that people held in James' day, even as they do in ours, that if we believe certain Bible doctrines intellectually, well, that is all that counts. According to this view, we do not have to live differently; our ethical life, our conduct or our behavior is irrelevant. The standards of living that Jesus sets before us do not matter so long as we believe that Jesus is God, that he died on the cross for sin, and that he rose again on the third day.

What is important about this, and tragic, is that many thousands of people in our churches today fit into this precise category. They believe the teachings of Christianity intellectually, and because they do – perhaps because of their own presumption in this area or in some cases because of the mistaken and unfortunate teaching of their pastors – they think they are basically right with God. James challenges this thinking, saying that the kind of faith through which we are saved is a living faith which is not mere intellectual assent to certain truths but a faith which expresses itself in good works and righteous actions.

Some time ago, when I was in Costa Rica, I heard Dr Paul Rees speak on 'world perspectives'. In one of these messages he told of a minister who had been engaging in an adulterous relationship with a woman of the congregation. When one of the elders discovered it, he approached the minister about it and asked him if it were true. The pastor replied that it was, but then added astonishingly, 'So what if I am committing adultery? I preach better sermons than I ever did.'

That man was saying, 'So long as I believe and teach the things that are in the Bible, it doesn't matter how I live.' But it does. James says it makes all the difference in the world, because if there is an indifference to sin, the faith which is assumed to be the basis of the individual's salvation is not a true, saving faith, and the individual is not a saved individual.

DEALING WITH BIBLE PROBLEMS

Before we consider this passage, however, let me ask a question. What is the best way for Christians to deal with a problem passage in the Word of God? Suppose you come upon a verse in your daily Bible reading that doesn't seem to make sense, or seems to contradict another passage you have read. What should you do with such a passage? Should you overlook it? Should you conclude that the Bible is simply full of contradictions? Or what?

Let me suggest this approach.

1. *Bring all the relevant facts to light.* That means that if this passage in James seems to contradict things that Paul says, the way to deal with the problem is not by suppressing one or the other of the passages but rather to consider both. If James says something, let us hear what James says; and if Paul says something, let us hear what Paul says.

2. *Compare those verses that touch on the problem.* This means that because Scripture is its own best and only infallible interpreter, we should compare Scripture with Scripture. We are to take the teachings of Paul that pertain to this theme and the teachings of James that pertain to this theme, put them side by side and study them to see what the true teaching is. When we do that, we may discover that the passages only seem to be contradictory but are actually in agreement. Or it may be the case, when we compare them, that we find that they are not teaching the same truth, but are teaching truths that complement one another. In other words, while they may not be teaching exactly the same doctrine, they may be teaching doctrines which are in overall agreement.

That is the case with this passage. James is emphasizing the importance of works. Paul emphasized faith. But if Paul were speaking on the same platform with James, they would not be debating with each other; they would be complementing each other.

3. *If necessary, suspend judgment.* What happens if having brought the facts to light and having compared Scripture with Scripture, you find that you still cannot make the truths either identical or complementary? What happens if they still seem to be contradictory? Then you must suspend judgment and wait for the

Lord to give you greater light at some later period of your development.

Dr Frank E. Gaebelein, in his brief commentary on the Epistle of James, told this story. Riding on a train along the Hudson river, a clergyman went into the dining car to eat and happened to seat himself next to a man who was an atheist. The clergyman was wearing his clerical collar, so the atheist knew his profession immediately.

'Are you a clergyman?' he asked.

'Yes, I am. I'm a minister of the gospel of Jesus Christ.'

'Well,' said the atheist, 'if that's the case, you must believe the Bible?'

'Yes, I do believe the Bible. I believe it's the Word of God, and that it's true.'

'But don't you find things in the Bible you don't understand?'

'Yes, there are many things in the Bible I don't understand,' the minister replied humbly.

The atheist thought he had the clergyman trapped. So he retorted triumphantly, 'Well, then, what do you do when you find things in the Bible you don't understand?'

While they had been talking the minister had been eating his dinner. It happened to be a Hudson river shad, noted for being very bony. He had been eating it carefully, pushing the bones to one side. He looked down at his plate for a moment. Then he said, 'Well, sir, I do precisely what I do when I'm eating this shad. I eat the good parts. But when I come to the bones I push them aside and leave them for some poor fool to choke on.'[1]

We may not express it exactly that way, but that is what we can

---

1. Frank E. Gaebelein, *The Practical Epistle of James: Studies in Applied Christianity* (Great Neck, NY: Channel Press, 1955) pp. 65, 66.

do too. There will always be things in the Bible that we do not understand. But after having brought the facts to light and having pursued the matter as carefully as we can, comparing Scripture with Scripture, if we still do not understand what we have read, we can simply suspend judgment and wait for God in his own time to give us more light.

FAITH THAT DOES NOT SAVE

Now let's look at this passage in James carefully. What is James really saying? The most important thing to notice is that James is describing not a true but a false faith, a faith that saves no one, and that he is contrasting it with a true faith that saves. The false faith that James is describing has several characteristics.

1. *It is merely intellectual.* It assents to certain truths, but it is not changed by them. James indicates that he is talking about this false kind of faith from the very beginning, in verse 14, where he asks, 'Can such faith save him?' When James adds the word 'such,' he is indicating that he is writing about a particular kind of faith, which we soon learn is a faith which is verbal only as opposed to being a true or living faith. In current English writing style, we would probably put the word 'faith' in quotation marks, asking, 'Can a "faith" like this save him?'

Again, James makes what he is doing clear by the phrase 'if a man claim to have faith but has no deeds?' This indicates that the faith he is discussing is a faith that exists on the basis of the claim only. That is, the person involved says he has faith but does not really have it.

In verse 19, James speaks about the faith of demons and, of course, this is also a faith that is simply intellectual. 'You believe that there is one God. Good! Even the demons believe that – and shudder.' You can imagine how ironic that must have sounded to those who first read this epistle. Here was someone in the fellowship of the church who was proud of the fact that he had faith. But James is saying to a person like that, 'If the only kind of faith you have is an intellectual faith, remember that it only brings you up to the level of the devils. You will have to go a great deal further than that to be saved.'

2. *It is ineffective.* This false faith that James is describing is also ineffective. It does nothing. It produces no results. In John 3, when our Lord talked about the Holy Spirit, who is invisible, he said the Holy Spirit was like the wind. 'The wind blows wherever it pleases. You hear its sound, but you cannot tell where it comes from or where it is going. So it is with everyone born of the Spirit' (v. 8). Jesus was teaching that although the Holy Spirit is invisible, he is nevertheless observable in his effects. In the same way, true faith is observable in its effects. False faith does not even rustle the leaves.

In contrast to this inadequate faith, James wants the real faith which he describes in verse 18. 'Someone will say, "You have faith; I have deeds." Show me your faith without deeds, and I will show you my faith by what I do.'

3. *It is useless.* In verse 20, James adds a third point, writing, 'You foolish man, do you want evidence that faith without deeds is useless?' Obviously, if a faith is useless in general, it is certainly useless in the matter of salvation.

4. *It is incomplete.* In verse 22, he talks about a faith that is incomplete. He is writing about Abraham at this point, and he notes of him, making a valid contrast, 'You see that his faith and his actions were working together, and his faith was made complete by what he did.'

5. *It is dead.* Finally, in both verses 17 and 26 James speaks of a faith that is dead. Clearly a dead faith will save nobody.

What is really bothering James is that this intellectual, ineffective, useless, incomplete and dead faith is without works. And when he is speaking about works, he does not mean the kind of works that arise out of our own corrupt natures, that Paul says God curses. He means rather the works that come out of the heart of a man or woman who has been reborn and has entered into a lifetime of obedient service based upon union with Jesus Christ. If such works are not present as an expression of our union with Christ, then James denies the reality of the union.

He gives a number of examples. In verses 15-17, he asks, 'Suppose a brother or sister is without clothes and daily food. If one of you says to him, "Go, I wish you well; keep warm and well fed," but does nothing about his physical needs, what good is it? In the same way, faith by itself, if it is not accompanied by action, is dead.'

I suppose we can read a passage like this and say, 'Yes I can understand that. It is certainly true. If one is to believe in Jesus Christ and follow him, there should certainly be an expression of compassion for other people in what he or she does.' But having acknowledged that intellectually, we can still go out and continue to ignore the needs of others. We must recognize that if there is a person who is hungry and we have the means of alleviating that hunger, we are not really Christians unless we help that person. That is what James is saying. This does not mean that in every particular case all down through our lives, whenever any need was presented to us, we had to meet that need as best we were able or we were not saved. But it does mean that we cannot be indifferent to need and still profess to be Christians. James is saying that if you are truly a Christian, you will increasingly show that kind of compassion to the needy that our Lord showed when he was here on earth. We must be concerned for others.

TRUE OR SAVING FAITH

It is one thing to say what faith is not, of course. It is quite another thing to say what faith is. What is a true faith? James would agree with Paul and all the great past theologians of the church, including Martin Luther, as expressing the nature of true faith by these three elements.

1. *Faith is based upon knowledge.* Faith that is merely intellectual is inadequate, as James has indicated. But this does not mean that true faith does not need content. To have faith means to believe. But how can you believe if you do not know what it is you are believing? So when we talk about Christian faith or saving faith, the first element of this faith is intellectual content expressed as the basic doctrines of Christianity. There is no such thing as saving faith that does not have knowledge of Jesus Christ as the eternal Son of God who became man and died on the cross for our salvation.

The ancient theologians of the church, who wrote in Latin, spoke of this element as *notitia*. It meant content.

2. *Faith involves our agreement with that content intellectually understood.* The older theologians called this assensus, meaning assent or concurrence. Sometimes it has been described as response or the warming of the heart towards what God has done. What is in view here is that reaction to God's grace in Jesus Christ that says, 'I acknowledge not only that Jesus died on the cross for the sin of men and women, but that he died on the cross for me. He died that I might be saved. Oh, what a gracious loving God, that he should do that for me!'

64

Remember that it is possible to understand the doctrine of justification intellectually – that God, on the basis of the righteousness of Jesus Christ, counts as righteous those who are not righteous in themselves but applies the righteousness of Christ to them on the basis of his death – and still be lost. You can understand this, as I say. But it is not enough merely to understand it. Added to the intellectual understanding must be the response that says, 'I agree that it is true, and I marvel that the great God of the universe should work out such a salvation for me!'

3. *Faith involves trust or commitment.* The older theologians called this fiducia. This element teaches that it is possible to have an intellectual understanding of the essential elements of Christianity followed by a certain stirring of the heart and yet at that point still be able to pull back from full trust in Christ or commitment to him. You might say, 'I believe it, but I still have my life to live. There are things that I'd rather do than be a Christian. Perhaps I'll give attention to religion at a later time.'

King Agrippa responded that way when he said to Paul, 'Paul, almost you persuade me to be a Christian' (Acts 26:28, KJV). His mind was touched. His heart was stirred. But he did not trust Christ. So he was not, nor did he become a Christian. True faith demands commitment. When we put these elements together, we usually summarize by saying that what is necessary is that a person receive Christ as his or her personal Saviour and Lord and that the person commits to follow Jesus as his disciple.

EXAMPLES OF FAITH

I am sure this is what James had in mind when he referred to Abraham in verse 21. James says that 'Abraham [was] considered righteous for what he did,' and later he quotes that great verse from Genesis 15 which says that Abraham 'believed' God and that this was 'credited ... to him as righteousness' (v. 6). So James is certainly not saying that Abraham was justified on the basis of his works and not by faith, thereby contradicting Paul. What he has in mind is this: Abraham believed God, and because he believed God he was willing to obey God when God commanded him to offer up his son Isaac. His obedience was evidence that he was indeed a regenerated person. If Abraham had refused to obey God, it would be right to question whether he actually believed God and was therefore saved at all.

James also gives the example of Rahab (v. 25). Rahab had been a prostitute in Jericho. She had a very limited knowledge of God, but when the spies came to Jericho preceding the Jewish conquest, she recognized them as messengers of the true God. That is, she believed on their God. Then she showed her belief by making her commitment to them and so saved the spies, delivering them from the city unharmed. For her faith she was later spared when the city was taken. James says, 'In the same way, was not even Rahab the prostitute considered righteous for what she did when she gave lodging to the spies and sent them off in a different direction?'

Once again, James is saying that a living faith will express itself in works. If there are no works, we have every reason to question the reality of the faith, no matter how loud a profession.

At the heart of it, this agrees with what Paul says in that magnificent summation of the way of salvation by grace through faith in Ephesians: 'For it is by grace you have been saved, through faith – and this not from yourselves, it is the gift of God – not by works, so that no one can boast' (Eph. 2:8, 9). That text affirms in language as strong as can possibly be devised that we are saved by the grace of God alone and that we receive this salvation by faith only. None of our own works can enter into justification. Yet Paul goes on to say in the next verse: 'For we are God's workmanship, created in Christ Jesus to do good works, which

God prepared in advance for us to do' (v. 10). In other words, just as we are ordained by God unto salvation, so are we ordained by God to do good works. So if the ordination is determinative in the first case, it must be determinative in the second. If the works are missing, true faith is missing also.

True Christianity always teaches that salvation is by faith alone. But it we are faithful to the whole Word of God, we must also add, as the Lutherans are in the habit of saying, 'We are saved by faith alone, but not by a faith that is alone.' A living faith expresses itself by works, that is, in a life that brings glory to Jesus Christ.

5

AT LEAST I'M NO HYPOCRITE!
(James 3:1-18)

All kinds of animals, birds, reptiles and creatures of the sea are being tamed and have been tamed by man, but no man can tame the tongue. It is a restless evil, full of deadly poison.

With the tongue we praise our Lord and Father, and with it we curse men, who have been made in God's likeness. Out of the same mouth come praise and cursing. My brothers, this should not be. Can both fresh water and salt water flow from the same spring? My brothers, can a fig tree bear olives, or a grapevine bear figs? Neither can a salt spring produce fresh water.

I f you are at all like me, I sense that after our last study of James 2:14-26 on the subject of faith issuing in good works, you rather wish that James would now talk about something 'theological' or 'spiritual'. I mean by this that his previous discussion of works was too personal. What we wish is that he would go on to something more abstract. We wish he would change the subject, because this is what we ourselves do. When we are involved in a conversation that becomes too personal, we try to change the subject. Or if we cannot do that, we try to keep it as theoretical as possible.

That is what the woman of Samaria did when Christ got too close to her. You remember how at one point in the conversation he asked her to go call her husband. He knew very well that she had no husband, that she was not really married. She was only living with a man. So she replied somewhat evasively, 'I have no husband.'

Jesus answered by getting to the heart of the matter. 'You are right when you say you have no husband. The fact is, you have had five husbands, and the man you now have is not your husband. What you have just said is quite true.'

At this point the conversation had become too personal, so she switched the subject to a theological area. She said, 'Sir, ... I can see that you are a prophet. [Now, since you are a prophet, perhaps you can answer this question that has been troubling me for some time. I want to know where a person should worship. Should we worship here in Samaria, as our priests say? Or should we worship in Jerusalem, as you Jews say?] Our fathers worshipped on this mountain, but you Jews claim that the place where we must worship is in Jerusalem' (John 4:16-20).

She changed the subject from being personal and practical to theoretical and impractical. There was not any chance in the world that she would actually go down to Jerusalem to worship. All she was trying to do was get the discussion off her personal life. Jesus knew what she was trying to do, of course. So he began to teach her and lead her to a proper relationship to himself.

That is what I am talking about here. When we come to a subject like faith and works and notice how practical James is when he deals with works, we wish we could get more 'theological'. It is because James' remarks are too direct for comfort. We would prefer him to discuss the nature of God or theories of the atonement. But James does not do that. Instead, he now writes what is probably the most practical section of the entire book, a part dealing with the tongue and the need for tongue control.

Tongue control? Yes, because this is something we struggle with every day of our lives. It is extremely practical.

THE TONGUE PROBLEM

What is the problem then? There are several problems actually. But the first problem James mentions is that, although the tongue is a small part of the body, it is nevertheless very effective in doing evil.

Our tongues can be used either for good or evil, of course. In history men have controlled nations through the force of their speech. One of the great orators of ancient times was Alcibiades of Athens. It was said that when he spoke he could get people to do anything. In modern times, we think of someone like Winston Churchill who rallied Great Britain to oppose the forces of Hitler's Germany by the force of his strong will and by his brilliantly persuasive speech. At the same time, however, we can also think of Adolf Hitler, on the other side of the channel, who used his oratorical ability to lead Germany into war. For a period of time he virtually enslaved Europe by the powers of the Axis war machine. He is a good illustration of what James is saying.

To make this graphic, James uses three illustrations. They are diverse illustrations, but they are alike in one thing: in each case a small thing has an impact on something much larger.

First, James speaks of a bit that is put in a horse's mouth. It is very small, just a few inches of steel or iron, yet it controls the horse. It turns the animal either to the right or left and makes it stop.

His second example is the rudder of a ship. It too is quite small, especially in comparison with the ship's great bulk. But when you turn it you can direct the motion of even the largest vessel.

James' third illustration is a spark. It too is small; yet this small spark can set an entire forest on fire and cause immense destruction.

These three illustrations are alike in their main point. Yet there are also significant small differences that contribute to the teaching. For example, a horse is a creature of great strength. Strength is a good thing, but unless strength is controlled it is ineffective. Again, a ship is of great value, able to transport people and merchandise. Yet if the rudder is not operating correctly, that merchandise may be transported to the wrong destination or the ship may even be destroyed. Without a reliable rudder, the valuable ship is worthless. Still further, a fire provides warmth and comfort to a home – if it is controlled. But uncontrolled, it is dangerous and becomes a source of almost unthinkable destruction.

We recognize the destruction the tongue of Adolf Hitler caused. But what we do not so easily admit is the damage that we do simply by an untimely word, an unfair evaluation or a small slander. We let words fall carelessly from our lips and seldom think twice about them. But in some cases they do damage that lasts a lifetime.

In his book *How to Win Friends and Influence People*, Dale Carnegie tells a story which illustrates the chief point of his book, namely, that you should never say anything bad about anyone. He recalls how a person once wounded him by a few words. This man was a writer of some repute. Carnegie wanted to be a writer too.

So he had written a letter to him to get some advice about writing. However, he did something he later realized was foolish. A short time before this he had received a letter from someone, and down at the bottom of the letter were the words 'Dictated, but not read'. It meant that the letter had been dictated by the person whose name was attached to it, but that this person had not had time to read it or sign it. The secretary had signed it for him. That seemed rather important to the young Carnegie. So, wanting to be important himself, Carnegie sent his letter with the same notation: 'Dictated but not read.'

The response he received was quite rude. The man to whom he had written did not even write back. He simply returned the letter, having scribbled over it: 'Young man, your bad manners are exceeded only by your bad manners.' Carnegie realized that he had been foolish, but the reply wounded him deeply. And twenty or more years later, when he picked up the newspaper one day and noticed this man's name in the obituary column, this was the incident that immediately came back to his mind.[1]

TONGUE CONTROL, MIND CONTROL

The second point James makes is that the tongue is uncontrollable. Are you surprised that he says this? I am. You would think that an apostle of the Lord, thinking of all that God is able to do, would say, 'The tongue may be very difficult to control, but God can help you control it.'

No doubt, James was well aware of the fact that spiritual resources are available to help us control our tongues. But that is not what he stresses in these verses. In this passage he was so carried away by his knowledge of what damage an uncontrolled tongue can do that he says the tongue is so bad that nobody

---

1. Dale Carnegie, *How to Win Friends and Influence People* (New York: Cardinal Books/Simon and Schuster, 1963), pp. 27, 28.

anywhere has ever been able to control it. 'All kinds of animals, birds, reptiles and creatures of the sea are being tamed and have been tamed by man, but no man can tame the tongue. It is a restless evil, full of deadly poison' (vv. 7, 8).

It is possible to infer that James is thinking here of other people's tongues, because it is certainly impossible to control what other people will say. You can lock your enemies up in a dungeon, and they will still shout obscenities at you. You can intimidate them when you are in their presence, but they will still talk about you behind your back. James may be thinking of how uncontrollable the tongues of other people are.

Still, I suspect that he is writing of something far more personal, since in the very next verse he goes on to say, 'With the tongue we praise our Lord and Father, and with it we curse men' (v. 9). This includes himself. So James must be thinking of himself and other Christians like him, and of the inability we all have to control our tongues. This is not merely a problem involving other men and women. That is what makes this so serious. We cannot control our own tongues. So if we are confronted with an impossibility such as tongue control, we obviously do need the help of God, with whom alone 'all things are possible'.

James says another thing about the tongue in verses 9 through 12. He says, 'With the tongue we praise our Lord and Father, and with it we curse men, who have been made in God's likeness. Out of the same mouth come praise and cursing. My brothers, this should not be. Can both fresh water and salt water flow from the same spring? My brothers, can a fig tree bear olives, or a grapevine bear figs? Neither can a salt spring produce fresh water.'

What does this mean? Well, in our terms it means that we go to church, sit there on a Sunday morning or evening and sing the hymns. Our spirits are lifted up. We are thinking, 'Oh, what a great God we have! How wonderful he is!' But then we go out of the church afterward and say, 'Did you see so-and-so? Why, when we were singing that hymn, he wasn't singing. I wonder what he is up to?' Or we say, 'Did you hear what I heard about so-and-so this morning? He's been cheating on his wife. That's terrible. I mustn't tell anybody about it, of course; and don't you tell anybody, unless you want to tell so-and-so, of course. But that's what is happening.'

James says that this is an unbelievable anomaly – good and evil coming out of the same mouth. You do not find it in nature. It runs against God's pattern in creation. A spring, he says, either sends forth good, clear water, or it sends forth bad water. You do not find the two mixed together. Similarly, a fig tree always produces figs, and a vine always produces grapes. Yet a Christian, who belongs to God and should speak the words of God, often speaks words that are destructive and harmful to other human beings. It ought not to be.

Of course, the explanation is not hard to find. It comes from the fact that we are still sinners even though we are saved. We still have an old nature, and the old nature is contrary to the things of God. It does not do what it ought to do, as Paul so clearly says in Romans. Consequently we need God's provision for our growth in this area.

The solution, as I have already intimated, is that, although with men tongue control is impossible, nevertheless, as Jesus said, 'With God all things are possible' (Matt. 19:26). You and I cannot control our tongues, but God by the power of his Holy Spirit within us can control them.

THREE HELPFUL PRINCIPLES

Let me give you three principles that I think will help. You might call them three steps to tongue control. They are based upon the fact that the tongue speaks what the mind thinks, so if we are to have tongue control, there must first of all be mind control.

1. *Present your mind to God.* In Romans 12:1, 2 the apostle Paul speaks of mind control. He does not mention speaking false or true things with the tongue in Romans 12, but these verses have bearing upon everything that follows: 'Therefore, I urge you, brothers, in view of God's mercy, to offer your bodies as living sacrifices, holy and pleasing to God – this is your spiritual act of worship. Do not conform any longer to the pattern of this world, but be transformed by the renewing of your mind. Then you will be able to test and approve what God's will is – his good, pleasing and perfect will.'

We do not usually think of our minds as parts of our bodies. But when Paul tells us to present our bodies to God for his service, the mind is the very first thing Paul thinks of. It is because he knew that if anything good is to develop in our lives, there must first be the transformation of our minds since what we think will always determine what we do. Moreover, it is only as we present our minds to God that we can be kept from thinking according to the world's standards. Only when we give our minds to God can they be channelled to think according to Christ's standards.

Frank E. Gaebelein wrote, 'Tongue control? It will never be achieved unless there is first of all heart and mind control.... Salvation applies to the whole man. The cleansing of the soul includes also the cleansing of the mind. When any Christian comes to the point of yielding to the Lord – in full sincerity, cost what it may – control of his thought life, the problem of managing his tongue will be solved, provided that such a surrender goes deeper than the intellect and reaches the emotions and the will. For the Bible makes a distinction between mere intellectual knowledge of God and the trust of the heart.'[2]

---

2. Frank E. Gaebelein, *The Practical Epistle of James: Studies in Applied Christianity* (Great Neck, NY: Channel Press, 1955), pp. 80, 81.

Have you surrendered your mind to God? In your own heart and mind, have you said to God, 'I am not my own; I know I belong only to you; do with me as you wish. Here is my mind. Here is my talent. Here is everything else I possess. These things are yours. Use them as you will; make them over into what you would have them be'? If you have not done that, you have not done the first thing. If you have, then God will begin to use that to bring about the tongue discipline (as well as other kinds of discipline) that you need.

2. *Begin to obey Christ's teachings.* Paul says in 2 Corinthians 10:5 that we have an obligation to bring every thought into obedience to Jesus Christ: 'We demolish arguments and every pretension that sets itself up against the knowledge of God, and we take captive every thought to make it obedient to Christ.' This means that there is no use saying, 'Well, God, I have given my mind to you. Here I am. Use me. Do anything you want,' and then not do anything about it ourselves. If we are serious about committing ourselves to Christ, then we must be serious about seeking out what Christ has said and striving to obey it. You are not Christ's unless you are obeying Christ, and you are not obeying if you do not pay attention to what Jesus taught.

Jesus said, 'Why do you call me, "Lord, Lord," and do not do what I say?' (Luke 6:46). It is a searching question. Do you confess Jesus to be your Lord and Savior? If so, do you do what he says?

As we begin to search the Scriptures to see what the Lord would have us do and then set about to obey it through the power of his Holy Spirit, God will begin to change our way of thinking. We will begin to think as he thinks. We will be starting to think the thoughts of God after God; and as we begin to think differently, we will begin to speak differently and the matter of tongue control will become a reality.

3. *Practice speaking helpfully.* Not only must we control our tongue negatively so that we do not say things we ought not to say; we must also control our tongue positively, so we say the things we ought to say. That will take conscious effort. It will require practice.

Why not set some personal goals in this area? You might determine to say one good thing in praise of God to someone every single day. You might decide to confess Jesus Christ as Lord in your life in some practical area. You might determine to memorize a Bible verse each week, so you can recite it to others. You might want to say something good about someone else. There are dozens of possibilities.

It may be helpful to remember that God tells us that he hears what we say and takes note of it himself. Toward the end of the Old Testament, in the third chapter of Malachi, we read that 'those who feared the Lord talked with each other [undoubtedly about the Lord], and the Lord listened and heard. A scroll of remembrance was written in his presence concerning those who feared the Lord and honored his name' (Mal. 3:16). If we use our tongues in a disciplined way to praise God, not with speech only but with the mind that goes behind it, God will bless our words and remember them and give us the ability to be a blessing to other people.

TRUE WISDOM

This chapter of James ends with a section on wisdom. It is a short section of only six verses, but I am sure James intended to connect it to the portion on the tongue, which we have been studying. James begins it by asking the question, 'Who is wise and understanding among you?' (v. 13). His answer, implied on the basis of the previous section, would be: 'The one who is able to control his tongue.'

But James continues by contrasting two kinds of wisdom: the wisdom of the world and the wisdom that is from heaven. The wisdom of the world seems wise and sophisticated and is that before which the knees of this world bow. Contrasted with it is the wisdom that comes from God. This wisdom may not call much attention to itself, but it is 'first of all pure; then peace loving, considerate, submissive, full of mercy and good fruit, impartial and sincere' (v. 17).

I realize that it is easy to be swept up by the very intellectual people of our world, who are apparently so brilliant and wise, and be tempted to say, 'Oh, I wish I had a mind like that.' Or, 'God, please give me wisdom like that.' But if James were here – although I do not think he would repudiate secular knowledge; truth is truth wherever you find it – I think he would say, 'Don't be too impressed by the world's wisdom. Ask, first of all, what kind of fruit is that kind of wisdom producing in the lives of those you think have it? Are these people who are at peace? Are they people who have a genuine inner joy? And when you have asked that, ask, What are these very wise people doing for other people?'

God's wisdom is the wisdom of Jesus Christ, who came and gave himself for us. Jesus gladly relinquished his rights in order that he might do good to others. He came not to be ministered unto, but to minister. He is our example. Peter speaks about this in the second chapter of his first epistle, saying, 'Christ suffered for you, leaving you an example, that you should follow in his steps' (I Pet. 2:21). There he calls upon us to set Christ before us as our example, showing that because he humbled himself, we should humble ourselves and serve others too.

I do not know how anything can be more practical than this. Yet at the same time, I do not know how anything can be more terrifying if we do not have the strength of God within. If we look to ourselves, none of us has the strength to do what God requires. But if we look to God for his help, then he will accomplish changes in our lives, and our words as well as what we do will be blessed to others.

6

IT'S HIS (HER) FAULT
(James 4:1-12)

What causes fights and quarrels among you? Don't they come from your desires that battle within you? You want something but don't get it. You kill and covet, but you cannot have what you want. You quarrel and fight. You do not have, because you do not ask God. When you ask, you do not receive, because you ask with wrong motives, that you may spend what you get on your pleasures.

IT'S HIS (HER) FAULT

I do not think I will ever write a psychology book, but if I did I would include a chapter on the disposition we all have to blame other people for our troubles. Several years ago comedian Flip Wilson invented a character called Geraldine, who was always saying, 'The devil made me do it.' It did not make any difference what she did. Whether she bought a dress she should not have purchased or whether she went somewhere she should not have gone, it was always the devil who made her do it.

Generally we are more sophisticated than that. In our contemporary, secular world where people do not even believe in the devil, we do not blame Satan. Instead, we blame other people. Hardly anything is more natural to us than our disposition to blame someone else for our own failures.

What happens when somebody is caught doing something wrong? Quite often the reply is: 'I wouldn't have done it if you hadn't done so-and-so.' Or, 'I do those things, because that's the way my father always acted.' It is always the other person's fault. Or the response may be, 'Well, maybe I shouldn't have done that, but you're just as bad.' Such a trait is easier to see in others than in ourselves, but if we are at all perceptive and honest, we have to admit that we too often use these tactics.

The apostle James had observed this tendency. Only he did not agree with our analysis. In the fourth chapter of his epistle he presents a very different picture. 'What causes fights and quarrels among you?' he asks. James answers, 'Don't they come from your desires that battle within you? You want something but don't get it. You kill and covet, but you cannot have what you want. You quarrel and fight. You do not have, because you do not ask God' (vv. 1, 2). James is saying that the basic problem is not what the other person is or does but rather what comes out of our own sinful hearts. No one needs to look further then himself or herself, because we, not other people, are the problem.

As he wrote these verses, James may have been thinking of the words of our Lord in Matthew 15. There, speaking of the ceremonial purifications of his day and the concerns people had to eat kosher foods, Jesus said that the things that defile a person are not what go into him but what come out. What comes out of the heart are 'evil thoughts, murder, adultery, sexual immorality, theft, false testimony and slander. These are what make a man "unclean"' (vv. 19, 20). This seems to be what James is thinking of. He recognizes that from our sinful nature come words and desires that bring about the trouble we see among men and women. So he asks, 'Don't [fights and quarrels] come from your desires that battle within you?' The answer, of course, is that they do. And for all of us.

WAR OUR CHIEF LEGACY

Some of our older versions translate James 4:1 with the words 'wars and fightings,' and this reminds us of how wars have characterized the history of the human race. They are one expression of the problem James is discussing. One commentator said that war is 'man's chief legacy,' meaning that it is the chief thing one generation most faithfully passes on to the next.

Each of the treaties of history has been hailed by someone at some time as the road to a just and lasting disarmament, but the ink had scarcely dried on most of these treaties when the guns began to sound for the next encounter. Gun powder, tanks, aeroplanes, missiles and nuclear weapons have been said to make war far too horrible to contemplate. But the experience of the race is that there is never a horror so great that someone will not use it to enforce his designs on others or others' possessions.

This judgment is not merely an expression of our own fading hopes for peace. It is vindicated by historical records. One of the earliest of all historical records, a Sumerian bas-relief sculpture from Babylon (c 3,000 BC), shows soldiers fighting in close order, wearing helmets and carrying shields. Wars fill the history of every ancient culture – Babylon, Syria, Assyria, Egypt, Phoenicia. The twenty-seven year-long Peloponesian War destroyed Greece even at the height of the great civilization she had created as the fruit of Athens' Golden Age. Rome made war a way of life, but even she was eventually defeated and overrun by the barbarians.

In the Middle Ages war ravaged Europe, culminating in the horrors of the Thirty Years War which ended in 1648. The Encyclopaedia Britannica calls the Thirty Years War 'the most horrible military episode in western history prior to the twentieth century'. By early estimates three fourths of the German-speaking peoples died in that war, but even by the more cautious estimate of destruction made later (only one third of the population) seven million people are judged to have lost their lives. We come to modern times, and we find that World War 1 was even more destructive. Approximately thirty million people perished in that war. People were horrified. But within a quarter of a century a similar war was fought in the same amphitheatre by the same parties and for much the same reasons. World War 2 resulted in the loss of sixty million lives, double that of the earlier conflict, while the costs quadrupled from an estimated $340 billion to an estimated $1 trillion.[1]

Since World War 2 there have been 'at least 12 limited wars in the world, 39 political assassinations, 48 personal revolts, 74 rebellions for independence, 1,162 social revolutions, either political, economic, racial, or religious'. So wrote *US News and World Report* in the December 25, 1967 issue. But by now the totals quite obviously need to be increased in each of those categories.

---

1. "War" in *Encyclopaedia Britannica*, vol. 23, pp. 198-202.

When we look at this long history of the world's wars, we recognize that it is a projection of the warfare that is within the human heart. Or to put it another way, it is a projection into history of my desire to have what I (or another) intensely want to have. That is what James is talking about in his analysis. He says, 'All of these troubles come because in our sin we desire our own pleasure at the expense of other people.'

Is there a solution? Yes. James gives it in verses 2 and 3: 'You kill and covet, but you cannot have what you want. You quarrel and fight. You do not have, because you do not ask God.' His solution is for us to give up struggling and instead ask God what his desires for us are.

ENEMIES OF GOD

As James continues to analyze this very practical problem, it is not merely the problems we have with other people that he has in view. True, we have those problems, but those are the problems that are only most apparent. We also have problems with God. So when James finishes writing about the problems we have with one another, he goes on to speak of our problems on that deeper level. He calls us 'adulterous people', because we have committed spiritual adultery against God. He speaks of a friend of the world being God's 'enemy'. What James has in mind here is the fact that we have rebelled against God's rightful rule over us and now fondly believe that we are masters of our own fate.

The word 'adulterous' reminds us of the Book of Hosea, which was written to show how people have rebelled against God. Hosea tells how God worked out a spiritual pageant in his life. He was to marry a wife who was going to prove unfaithful to him. Hosea was to represent God. His adulterous wife was to represent the people of Israel, because, as God said, 'My people have been unfaithful to me. I have taken them to myself, but they have run away with other gods. They have been spiritual adulterers.'

'Moreover,' said God, 'instead of being ashamed of what they have done, they are actually proud about it. They boast of their achievement.'

In this spiritual pageant, the time came when Hosea's wife left him for another man, and in time she passed from that man to another man and then to another. Finally, she sank so low in the social scale of that age that she became a slave, probably for debt. At that point God told Hosea to go to the market place and buy her. So he did. He bid fifteen pieces of silver and a homer and a lethek of barley. The auctioneer sold her to Hosea, and Hosea took her to himself. He could have killed her if he had wanted to do that, because now she belonged to him. But instead of that he pledged his love to her while, at the same time, claiming no less from her. He told her, 'You are to live with me many days; you must not be a prostitute or be intimate with any man, and I will live with you' (Hos. 3:3).

So it is that God loves us. Hosea's purchase of his wife is a vivid illustration of God's purchase of us by Christ's death on Calvary. He bought us at the price of his blood, and now we must live for him. One of our hymns rightly says,

Love so amazing, so divine
Demands my soul, my life, my all.

And it does. It is this amazing love of Almighty God for us that makes our spiritual adultery such a terrible sin and heinous crime.

In verses 7 and 8 James speaks of a cure for this adultery against God, just as earlier he had pointed out a cure for the problem between ourselves and other persons. James says, 'Submit yourselves, then, to God. Resist the devil, and he will flee from you. Come near to God and he will come near to you.'

How do we draw near to God? Is James saying that the first move is up to us? If we seek God, then God will seek us? No, that is not what James is saying at all.

We draw near to God at the cross, and we draw near to God as the Holy Spirit draws us to him. It would be correct to say that as God has drawn near to us, so God draws us to himself. 'Submit to God' means 'submit to the drawing power of God'. If you do this, if you allow God to draw you to himself, you will find God to be the one you need. He will restore the broken Creator/creature relationship and subdue your pride.

This is the truth that Isaac Watts conveyed in his great hymn of the atonement.

When I survey the wondrous cross
On which the Prince of glory died,
My richest gain I count but loss,
And pour contempt on all my pride.

Submission to God happens in no other way and in no other place, for only as we see what God has done for us is our pride subdued and we find ourselves being brought near to him.

So long as we think we are contributing spiritually to what God is doing, we will be proud of what we have done. But when we see the matter as God portrays it in Scripture, when we see the cross, we will recognize how desperate our state is and that there is nothing in us to commend us to God. We are the kind of men and women who crucified Jesus. Yet God still sent his Son to pay the price of our sin and then by the power of his Spirit open our eyes to see what we have done and draw our wills so that we might come and receive the Lord Jesus Christ as our Saviour.

When we recognize what God has done for our salvation, we are truly humbled and are able to ask God to do with us what needs to be done.

DEFEATING TEMPTATION

In verse 7 James speaks of resisting the devil. So we need to think about temptation. In chapter one James wrote of two different kinds of temptation, one of which is more properly interpreted as testing. God himself sometimes brings testing into the lives of his people for their good. This is not a temptation to sin but a testing by which we are made strong. The kind of testing God brought into the life of Abraham in asking him to sacrifice his son is an example. It was not to get Abraham to sin, but rather to test Abraham so that he might grow in faith. Indeed, his faith did grow, and he is praised for it in Hebrews 11:17-19. That is one kind of testing or temptation.

On the other hand, there is a temptation which is not at all a testing for good but rather is a temptation to do evil. James also refers to this in chapter one. This is not of God. It comes from one of three sources: 1) from our own hearts; that is, it is a temptation of the flesh; 2) from the world and its values; or 3) from the devil.

I refer to this here because in this fourth chapter James is clearly talking about all three sources of temptation. In verses 1-3, when he speaks of fights and quarrels that come forth out of the heart of man, he is speaking of fleshly temptations, those which come from within ourselves. In verse 4, when he speaks of friendship with the world and a corresponding hatred toward God, he is speaking of temptations that come from the world and its values. Finally, in verse 7, he is speaking of temptation that comes to us directly from Satan.

The question is: If temptation is all around (both without and within), how are we to overcome it?

I want to suggest something. Just as there are three sources of temptation – from the flesh, the world and the devil – so also there are three ways of resisting temptation, with a different biblical approach for each one.

1. *Resisting temptations of the flesh.* What does Scripture say about dealing with fleshly temptations? Well, in I Corinthians 6:18 Paul says, 'Flee from sexual immorality.' Clearly sexual immorality is a fleshly temptation, and the advice Paul gives is to flee from it. He says the same thing in another place: 2 Timothy 2:22. Here Paul is writing to his young son in the faith, and he says, 'Flee the evil desires of youth.' That is, run away from fleshly temptations. Usually we think it is ignoble to run away from something. We think we should stand up and fight. But in regard to fleshly temptations, the Bible advises us to flee, obviously because we are not strong enough in ourselves to resist them. Joseph did this in regard to Potiphar's wife when he fled from her, leaving his garment in her hands.

What are fleshly temptations? Most people naturally think of sexual temptation exclusively, and certainly that is one kind. But overeating is another. Drunkenness is a third. The only way to overcome these things is to run away from them.

Suppose a young man and a young woman are getting sexually involved. They are alone in an apartment. How are they going to avoid going too far? Well, they do not overcome it by sitting down to reason it out rationally. What they have to do is to get out of the apartment. They have to go somewhere else and do something else. Similarly, if you have a problem with overeating, you have to push your chair away from the table, get up and leave the dining room. If you have a problem with drinking, you must avoid bars. If you have a problem with sexual perversions, and other problems in the sexual area, avoid the places where these temptations come to you. You have to feed yourself with what is wholesome and builds up and not with what has been tearing you down.

2. *Resisting temptations from the world.* What about the temptations that come to us from the world. The solution in this area is found in Romans 12:2, where Paul says, 'Do not conform any longer to the pattern of this world, but be transformed by the renewing of your mind. Then you will be able to test and approve what God's will is – his good, pleasing and perfect will.' The problem here is the world's value system. It presses in upon us on all sides. So almost without thinking we find ourselves being pushed into it. If the world values wealth, we begin to value wealth also. If the world values prestige, we begin to value prestige. When we read magazines, when we watch television, when we hear people talk, the values we see or hear in those places and from those sources tend to become our values.

The only way to overcome the desire to be like the world is by an inward transformation of the mind as you feed upon the Word of God, fellowship with Christian people, stay in communion with God and work out in your life what that good, pleasing and perfect will of God is. The world tells us that its way is good, pleasing and perfect and that anybody who does not go its way is foolish. But God says that the values of the world are a dangerous mirage, leading down a dark tunnel. You have to discover that it is really the will of God that is good. It is good, because God is good and because he is the source of all good. It is pleasing, pleasing both to us and to God, because it always works out well in the long run. It is perfect, because neither we nor anybody else can improve on it.

3. *Resisting the devil.* Although there are temptations that come directly from the devil, most of us are probably not tempted directly by the devil. This is because the devil is a created being. He is not omnipresent, and therefore he cannot be in every place tempting everyone at once. He can extend the sphere of his temptations through the demons who fell with him, but they cannot be in every

place tempting everyone either. Probably the devil does not consider it necessary to tempt most of us personally since we succumb so readily to the temptations of the flesh and the world without him. He does not need to waste time on us.

Nevertheless, if he does tempt us, the way to overcome his temptations is by resisting him, and we do that, first of all, by submitting to God, and, second, by resisting Satan directly, as the text says.

What does it mean to submit? And what does it mean to resist? We have no better example than that of the Lord Jesus Christ himself. Before he was tempted in the wilderness Jesus had spent forty days fasting and in prayer. That is, he had been submitting himself to God and seeking God's way. Then, when the devil came to him, he replied not in the words of the world but rather in the words of Scripture, quoting three times from the Book of Deuteronomy: 'Man does not live on bread alone, but on every word that comes from the mouth of God' (Matt. 4:4; see Deut. 8:3); 'Do not put the Lord your God to the test' (Matt. 4:7; see Deut. 6:16); 'It is written: "Worship the Lord your God, and serve him only"' (Matt. 4:10; see Deut. 6:13).

That is what it means to submit and to resist. It means to prostrate oneself before God in prayer, desiring his will, asking to go in his way and feeding upon his Word. Then, having that Word so much a part of our thinking, that when the devil's temptation comes, we reply not by saying, 'Well, let's see now, is this something I want to do, or isn't it?', but rather by rejecting it instantly on the basis of the biblical revelation, knowing what the Bible teaches.

If we do that, we will stop blaming other people for our troubles. We will see where the fault lies, and there will be a natural self-correction which will cause us to grow spiritually.

Once there was a little girl named Susie. Susie beat up her brother, and her mother punished her by making her stand in the corner. As the mother put her in the corner, she asked, 'Susie, why did you allow the devil to put it into your head to punch your brother, pull his hair and kick his shins?' Susie thought it over a minute, then said, 'Well, maybe the devil did put it into my head to punch him and pull his hair, but kicking his shins was my own idea.' Susie was a perceptive theologian.

7

HOW MUCH INSURANCE
DO I NEED?
(James 4:13-17)

Now listen, you who say, 'Today or tomorrow we will go to this or that city, spend a year there, carry on business and make money.' Why, you do not even know what will happen tomorrow. What is your life? You are a mist that appears for a little while and then vanishes. Instead, you ought to say, 'If it is the Lord's will, we will live and do this or that.' As it is, you boast and brag. All such boasting is evil. Anyone, then, who knows the good he ought to do and doesn't do it, sins.

HOW MUCH INSURANCE DO I NEED?

So far as I know, there were no insurance companies in New Testament times. But I have called this chapter, 'How Much Insurance Do I Need?' because I think our contemporary concern for insurance parallels the anxious self-provision that James describes in the last paragraph of chapter 4.

If you listen to the insurance companies, the question, 'How much insurance do I need?' is unanswerable, for you are almost always urged to buy more. In fact, it has become a cliché in the insurance business that you can never have too much insurance. Anything can happen. The factory can burn down. Employees can be hurt on your time and sue for enormous sums of money. People can break into your home and destroy it. You may get sick. Your grandmother may get sick. You may die. You never know what is going to take place. Therefore, the more insurance you have the better off you will be, since in the world's analysis security comes only from money.

This is the situation the insurance companies want to project, too. I think, for example, of the logo of All-State Insurance: those four wonderful hands joined together in an insurance bond. Wouldn't you like to be held up and supported by a group of people like that?

Or there is the Century Insurance Company whose logo is a Minute Man. Wouldn't you like one of those to fight your battles and defeat your enemies? You would. In fact, you would prefer the whole militia. You would be especially glad to have it if the Hartford Company came around with its logo, an elk, because a Minute Man could get that big animal off your lawn. He could shoot it!

Perhaps best of all is the John Hancock Company that has the rock of Gibraltar as its symbol. What could be more secure than that?

What indeed?

In chapter 4 James reminds those to whom he is writing that any attempt to find security apart from God is an illusion.

ILLUSION OR REALITY

Now, please, I am not opposed to insurance. Insurance policies are helpful when disasters occur, and owning a certain amount of insurance is prudent. In some cases it is even required by law. But if James were living today, he would say, 'If you think your real security comes from anything you can do for yourself, you are very much deceived, since in the ultimate analysis, life is uncertain at best and security only comes from God.' The example James gives is that of travelling merchants. These people might have supposed that their security came from getting as rich as they could get. They had the ability to make money, and making money gave them capital. So they traveled from city to city, selling their goods and making money. Eventually they hoped to return home with so much money they would be set for life. But hoping to find security in this way is an illusion.

Here is the way James talks about it: 'Now listen, you who say, "Today or tomorrow we will go to this or that city, spend a year there, carry on business and make money." Why, you do not even know what will happen tomorrow. What is your life? You are a mist that appears for a little while and then vanishes' (v. 14).

Do you see James' point? He is speaking to people who were trusting in human security, and he is saying, in effect, no matter how much insurance you have it is ultimately unreliable. What you really need is to turn your life over to God who alone is totally reliable. The picture James gives is of a fog which seems substantial when it is thick, yet disappears quickly as soon as the sun is up. Life is like that, he says. You cannot guarantee your life, even for a moment, and life is what all people prize most highly. So if you cannot guarantee your life, how can you suppose that you can guarantee anything that life holds?

At this point we are reminded of the man Jesus talked about who thought he would provide for himself by building bigger and better barns. He had an abundant harvest. So he said, 'This is what I'll do. I will tear down my barns and build bigger ones, and there I will store all my grain and my goods. And I'll say to myself, "You have plenty of good things laid up for many years. Take life easy; eat, drink and be merry."'

The Lord said of this man, 'You fool! This very night your life will be demanded from you. Then who will get what you have prepared for yourself?' (Luke 12:18-20).

The author of Proverbs was thinking along the same lines when he wrote:

Do not boast about tomorrow,
for you do not know what a day may bring forth (Prov. 27:1).

TWO GREAT ERRORS

But planning for the future and trying to insure ourselves against any possible disasters is so common that we have to think carefully if we are to discover what about this particular approach is wrong. Let me suggest two things.

1. *We forget that life is now.* The man depicted by James is living for the future to such an extent that he has no real regard for the present. He has forgotten that life is now. I remember many things that I was taught by my parents as I was growing up, but one thing my mother said will always be particularly remembered. She said, 'When you're young, you're always looking to the future. You are always thinking about what will happen or what you will do then. Don't forget that your life is now. Today is your life.' That has stuck with me.

It is true, of course, that we have an obligation to plan for the future in some areas. We need to provide for our family. We should lay aside money for retirement. There are many things that require prudent planning. Still, there is a sense in which our life really is now. So if you are not living for the Lord Jesus Christ *now* – if you are not living a full Christian life *now*, if you are not being used by God in the lives of other people *now* – who is to say that your life will ever be used by God in those areas?

2. *We forget about God.* The second thing that was wrong with the people about whom James is writing is that they were planning for the future without thinking of God. As I said, a certain amount of planning is prudent and probably necessary. But the only planning that makes full sense for Christian people is the planning that takes God into account. It is not the planning that says, as these merchants did, 'Tomorrow we are going to go here and do this, and after that we'll do something else in order to get richer; then we will be more comfortable, happier.' The planning that makes sense for Christian people always asks, 'What does God will?'

James raises the question in verse 15: 'Instead, you ought to say, "If it is the Lord's will, we will live and do this or that."' When you direct your attention to God with this in mind, you think not only of God prolonging life but also of the way he wants to prolong it, that is, what he wants you to do with the life he's given you.

This has practical implications. For one thing, it humbles us because it causes us to recognize our dependence upon God. Life is from God. God has given it, and God will take it away. Prosperity is a gift of God. God gives it, and God can take it away.

If we have any doubts about that, we have only to consider Job. Job was a prosperous and upright man. We know he was upright, because God testified concerning Job, 'Have you considered my servant Job? There is no one on earth like him; he is blameless and upright, a man who fears God and shuns evil' (Job 1:8). Yet in a moment Job lost everything. His livestock was either destroyed or carried off by robbers. His children were killed while eating together in the oldest brother's house. Even Job's health was destroyed. Job's story reminds us that all we have is from God, and anything we have can be taken by God. The man who does not remember this is foolish.

THE SIN OF FORGETTING GOD

The attitude of the merchants was also sinful. Indeed, this is the way the passage concludes: 'As it is,' James says, 'you boast and brag. All such boasting is evil. Anyone, then, who knows the good he ought to do and doesn't do it, sins' (vv. 16, 17). The attitude that says, 'I will provide for myself,' is sinful because it forgets that God is the one who has provided for us and the one upon whom our security ultimately depends. That attitude is really a kind of selfish self-aggrandizement.

It was the sin of Satan, who said in utter disregard of God and God's prerogatives,

'I will ascend to heaven;
I will raise my throne
above the stars of God;
I will sit enthroned on the mount of assembly,
on the utmost heights of the sacred mountain.
I will ascend above the tops of the clouds;
I will make myself like the Most High'   (Isa. 14:13, 14).

Satan said, 'I will go up, up, up.' But God said, 'You are brought down to the grave, to the depths of the pit' (v. 15). To aspire to anything without thinking to please God is a sin of which we need to repent. It is a sin for which we need to ask God's forgiveness.

'IF GOD WILLS'

Let me ask this question: If planning for ourselves and our future without accounting for God is the wrong attitude, what should the right attitude be?

The first answer is seen in verse 15, where James writes, 'You ought to say, "If it is the Lord's will, we will live and do this or that."' Before we plan, we should seek the will of God in the planning. I suppose that if James were amplifying this, he would probably say that if we seek the Lord's will, then some of the plans we have had for ourselves before we sought the will of God will change.

This should challenge us to rigorous thinking. For most of the western world a person's reasonable life-ideal is prosperity. We seek material prosperity, going from job to job, and step up the ladder of success as far as we can possibly go. Is that biblical? Is that Christian? Is that the life that is held out before us in the gospel?

I am not suggesting that Christians are to be mediocre in their work. Certainly if we are given talents, we should develop them to the full. If we are to be doctors, we should be the best doctors we can possibly be. If we are in the insurance business, we should be the best insurance agents we can be. If we are preachers, we should be the best preachers we can be. But there is a difference between doing the best we can with what God has given us and that basically secular western idea that says, 'What I have to do is work my way to the top as quickly as possible for my own gain.'

If we seek God's will regarding our jobs, I think that in many cases we will not take the best-paying job that is offered to us. There will be other factors involved. In some cases we might even move out of one business into another business, because the first is requiring us to compromise our Christian commitment, even though it may mean moving to a lower paying position.

Some time ago I knew a young man who was facing such a decision. Though he had a good job and was happy in it, he had been offered another job which was much more lucrative. Along with the new job would come increased prestige. Yet he was troubled by the prospect because it would involve doing things he did not want to do as a Christian. In the final analysis, as he sought the will of God and prayed about it, he decided to decline the job that was more lucrative. If we seek the Lord's will, our choices will usually be different from what the world would choose in the same situation.

We cannot say what decisions another person should be making, of course. We must not become 'know-it-alls' where other people are concerned. Each person must answer to his or her Master individually. But that means that we must do it too; and in order to answer to God well, we must ask God what his will for us is. Remember that God may direct you to use your talents, even talents of an extraordinary nature, in humble surroundings and for the good of very simple people.

DON'T WORRY

Second, our attitude should be characterized by great trust in God. It may be that once again James has a passage from the Sermon on the Mount in mind. In Matthew 6 our Lord was speaking about worry. He had already talked about money and had made a sharp contrast between serving God and money. Now he turned to those who were thinking, 'Well, if I don't concern myself with money, how am I going to take care of myself?' and he showed how instead of worrying about money we are to trust God.

The outline of this section (Matt. 6:25-34) is very interesting. The King James Version makes it especially clear by using the word 'therefore' three times: once in verse 25, once in verse 31, and a third time in verse 34. The idea is: 1) Therefore, don't worry; 2) Therefore, don't worry; and 3) Therefore, don't worry. (The New International Version only uses the word 'therefore' twice, though it uses the word 'so' in virtually the same sense in verse 31.)

When you have that many 'therefores' you have to ask what they are 'there for,' and when you do that here, you begin to see what the Lord is saying. Each time the word occurs, it refers to something that went before, and what comes before is the reason for the conclusion. Since each of the verses introduced by the word 'therefore' says, 'Don't worry,' what you have in the verses before them are three reasons why we are not to worry but instead are to trust God.

1. *Because you cannot trust both God and money.* In verse 24 Jesus is talking about two masters. He says, 'No-one can serve two masters. Either he will hate the one and love the other, or he will be devoted to the one and despise the other. You cannot serve both God and Money.' Verse 25 then concludes, 'Therefore ... do not worry.' The point is that if above all things you are concerned with providing for yourself and therefore direct all your attention to accumulating this world's goods, you cannot also be loving God or trusting him; you cannot do both together. This does not mean – I repeat it again – that a person cannot trust God and go about his business in a reasonable way. But he must be serving God! If you are worrying about this world's things, you are not trusting God.

You know the little Christian cliché: If you are worrying, you are not trusting; and if you are trusting, you are not worrying. It is true. We learn from Matthew 6:24 that Jesus is the author of it.

2. *Because God is able to provide for you.* In verse 31 Jesus again says, 'Don't worry,' and again the reason given is in the preceding verses. These speak of God's ability to provide for us. They refer to the birds of the air and the lilies of the field. Jesus reasons, 'If God cares for birds and even flowers, obviously he is able to care and will care for you.'

The first argument was an appeal to *reason*, you see. Jesus said, in effect, 'Think it over. If you're worrying, you're not trusting;

if you're trusting, you're not worrying. It can't be any other way. Use your mind.' This second argument appeals to our powers of *observation*. It says, 'Just look about you at the world. God made the world. God provides for it. The birds are provided for; the lilies are provided for. Doesn't it follow from what you can observe in nature that God is certainly able and will take care of you?' Surprisingly, we look at the world God made and say, 'Yes, he does take care of the birds; he does take care of the lilies; he does take care of the animals.' But we add, 'I still don't think he can take care of me!' The Lord says that is foolish. Birds and flowers are valuable. God made them. But human beings are still the peak of the created order, and they are even more valuable. God will certainly care for us.

3. *Because trusting God works.* Finally, in verse 34, Jesus has his third 'therefore', and once again the reasoning is in the verse preceding it: 'Seek first his [God's] kingdom and his righteousness, and all these things will be given to you as well.' What kind of an argument is this? Well, if the first argument was logical, appealing to reason, and the second argument was based on simple observation, this argument has to do with *experience*. Jesus is saying, 'If you don't believe what I am saying, check it out. Try it and see if it doesn't work. Put God first and see if God will not provide for you in all these other areas as well.'

Now, to be perfectly honest, we have to say that the way God provides for us is not always the way we would choose to provide for ourselves. And certainly it is not the way we would choose to provide for ourselves when we are thinking along worldly lines. We think we would like to have a mansion. Or we would like to have millions of dollars in a bank account. God does not promise to provide for such wants, and it is very, very rare when God does provide his people with such things. Yet God still provides. He provides for our needs. If you put God and his concerns first, if you seek his righteousness and make it your goal to live for him as one characterized by the priorities and morality of Jesus Christ, God will provide for your many needs and bless you in other ways you have not even thought of yet.

I began this chapter by referring to ads from the insurance companies. At this point I am reminded again of the Prudential advertisement offering a piece of the rock. Would you like a piece of the rock? What could be more reassuring than to own a piece of the Rock of Gibraltar?

Well, there is something more secure, and that is to be built on the Rock of Ages, on the One who changes not, on God who stands by his promises and is able to do what he has promised and will surely do it now and until the end of time.

In one of the early Greek manuscripts from the first centuries of the Christian era, there is a record of a man whose name was Titedios Amerimnos. The first part of that name is a proper name, but the second part is made up of the Greek word for 'worry' plus the prefix meaning 'not' or 'never'. In other words, the second part of the name is a descriptive epithet like the second part of 'Frederick the Great' or 'James the Just'. In this case many have thought that the man was originally a pagan who constantly worried but who, after he became a Christian, stopped worrying. He was then called Titedios Amerimnos – 'Titedios, the man who never worries.' Can you add that epithet to your name? You should be able to write 'John Smith ...', 'Betty Jones ...', 'Charles Miller ...', 'Susan Moore ...' (or whatever your name may be) and then add, 'the one who never worries'.

8

'BELIEVE ME, RICH IS BETTER'
(James 5:1-6)

Now listen, you rich people, weep and wail because of the misery that is coming upon you. Your wealth has rotted, and moths have eaten your clothes. Your gold and silver are corroded. Their corrosion will testify against you and eat your flesh like fire. You have hoarded wealth in the last days. Look! The wages you failed to pay the workmen who mowed your fields are crying out against you. The cries of the harvesters have reached the ears of the Lord Almighty. You have lived on earth in luxury and self-indulgence. You have fattened yourselves in the day of slaughter. You have condemned and murdered innocent men, who were not opposing you.

Whenever I come to the fifth chapter of James, I think of that often-quoted remark of Sophie Tucker: 'I've been rich and I've been poor and, believe me, rich is better.'

That is not what James is saying in his epistle, however, because according to Scripture, riches are neither good nor evil in themselves; they are morally neutral. At the same time, riches present a great danger. It is not biblical to say that being rich is better than being poor any more than saying that being poor is better than being rich. God is in charge of all things, and he sometimes gives one person the blessing of poverty just as he gives another person the blessing of wealth. Instead of either glorifying riches or deprecating them we should regard them in much the same way as we regard fire. Fire can be either good or bad. It can warm or destroy. It is useful, but it is also dangerous. It is just that way with riches.

CHAPTER TWO AND CHAPTER FIVE

James had talked about riches previously in chapter two, and it is good to keep that in mind as we look at chapter five. In chapter two he was talking about that wrong and sinful deference within Christian circles whereby preference is given to some people because they have money. In that passage he was referring to Christians, presumably rich and poor Christians within the fellowship of the church. He was not condemning wealth or wealthy Christians. He was simply condemning this deferential attitude, because it is a wrong way to act within the body of Christ.

In chapter five he again talks about riches, but now he is not referring to Christians who have money; he is speaking rather of the ungodly and their wealth. In this passage, James' words are as strong as those of any of the Old Testament prophets who denounced the ungodly rich of their day or of any of today's prophets who speak about the oppression that people in positions of authority sometimes inflict on those who are less fortunate. He denounces those who cheat others in order to have more money for themselves.

'Now listen, you rich people, weep and wail because of the misery that is coming upon you. Your wealth has rotted, and moths have eaten your clothes. Your gold and silver are corroded. Their corrosion will testify against you and eat your flesh like fire. You have hoarded wealth in the last days. Look! The wages you failed to pay the workmen who mowed your fields are crying out against you. The cries of the harvesters have reached the ears of the Lord Almighty. You have lived on earth in luxury and self-indulgence. You have fattened yourselves in the day of slaughter. You have condemned and murdered innocent men, who were not opposing you.'

WARNING TO THE UNGODLY RICH

As we look at those verses we can hardly miss James' emphasis. He is looking at a great wrong and is saying that God notices the wrong. In the Psalms we read of wicked people who said, 'No one pays any attention to what I do. Even the Lord doesn't see. I can do what I wish. God doesn't judge me.' In response to such a secular attitude, the Psalmist says (as James also does here) that although judgment has not yet come, the day of reckoning is nevertheless certain. God notices what is happening, and he is determined to judge injustice by his standards.

We need to remember that God notices what is going on. We may be able to hide our wickedness or the way we use our money from other people on occasion, but we cannot hide it from God. Notice what God sees.

1. *Withholding wages.* God notices those who are not paying their workmen sufficient wages, or not paying them at all, and he doesn't

like it. God has a concern for fair wages. He regards as sin any failure to pay or any underpaying of workmen.

2. *Self-indulgence and luxury.* These harm the poor, not because the wealth of one man necessarily hurts another, but because over-indulgence squanders what could be used to help others. James is saying that those who are rich should indulge themselves less and use some of that money to help those (or even pay the wages of those) who are less fortunate.

3. *Specific acts of evil.* God notices that the rich have 'condemned and murdered' innocent men. Some writers think that James is speaking here of the prophets, and that may be right. Certainly the prophets were innocent men who spoke against injustices and often were slain as a result. However, in the very last phrase of verse 6, James says, 'You condemned and murdered innocent men who were not opposing you.' Since the prophets did oppose the system, James must be referring here to people who were mere victims of the system. He is saying that when these die, as many do in poverty because of oppression, those who failed to pay them just wages are guilty not merely of neglecting the needs of such persons but of murder.

These are serious words, and we have to admit that in our own extremely materialistic and selfish society they can be applied in many areas and to many people very, very directly.

WHAT IS THE PROBLEM?
Is it wrong to possess material goods, then? No, that is not the case, because when we go back to the early chapters of Genesis we find that God prepared a whole world of things for the enjoyment of the first man and woman. In fact, he gave the entire world as their possession. They were to possess it and rule it

wisely. They were not to strip the world of its bounty for their own ends, but it was theirs nevertheless. Adam and Eve were to eat of the fruit of the garden; they were to enjoy the vistas of the creation. 'Things' were not wrong in themselves.

Someone might say, 'Well, that may have been true back there in Genesis before the Fall when the world was not corrupted by sin. But today, after the Fall, the possession of things is wrong.' People have argued this from time to time, and some have tried to develop an ascetic life where they give away their possessions. Moreover, they have encouraged others to do this and have set up monastic or monastic-like orders in which men and women have been encouraged to live apart from the rest of civilization, believing the possession of any worldly goods to be wrong. God may lead some people to enter this way of life, of course, but I do not believe it can be justified biblically as an ideal. Besides the possession of worldly wealth or goods is not wrong.

Let me point you to some Scripture. The eighth commandment says, 'You shall not steal' (Exod. 20:15). That commandment condemns theft. But not only does that commandment say that I should not steal from other people, it is also saying that other people should not steal from me. In other words, indirectly it establishes the right of private property.

What does this mean specifically? Well, it means that burglars should not steal, of course. But it also means that owners should not steal from their employees by not paying them sufficiently, the evil James is exposing and condemning. It means that employees should not steal by wasting company time or using the company's raw products for themselves. It could also be extended to mean that government should not steal from its people by extra high or confiscatory taxation. There are all kinds of applications. What is basic in all this is the right to private property.

Let me give another text. In the early church there was a period when the Christians in Jerusalem sold their possessions and deposited their wealth in a common treasury so there would be sufficient for all who might have need. We are told that 'all the believers were together and had everything in common' (Acts 2:44). Some have called that communism and have viewed it as an example of what they would like to see all Christians do today. They would encourage Christians to give everything away and live on communes.

Perhaps some Christians are called to that life style. That is between themselves and the Lord. But we have to note that just two verses further on in Acts 2, we are told that the Christians worshipped in one another's homes (v. 46). So while many may have sold their possessions and then have given the money to the church in this particular period of church history, some at least still had private homes. And those who were living communally did not consider the ones who still had homes to be disobeying God's commandments. Rather, they accepted what God had given as the blessing it was and then met in these private homes, making this common worship experience part of their witness to the people of Jerusalem.

Here is another situation. Ananias and Sapphira were two Christians living at the time when many were selling what they had and bringing the money they received from the sale to the apostles. Ananias and Sapphira went through these motions too, but they were not honest about it. After they had sold a piece of property, they kept part of the money for themselves. Then they took the rest and gave it to Peter, saying, 'We have sold a piece of property, and we are giving the proceeds to God.'

You know what happened. First, Ananias was struck dead by God, and then his wife Sapphira, since she was in on the deception too.

Peter, who was in charge and was God's spokesman on this

occasion, explained the reason for the judgment. The reason for their deaths was not the fact that Ananias and Sapphira had private property and had refused to give it up, but rather their hypocrisy in pretending to have given everything to God when, in fact, they had not done so. Peter said, 'Ananias, how is it that Satan has so filled your heart that you have lied to the Holy Spirit and have kept for yourself some of the money you received for the land? Didn't it belong to you before it was sold? And after it was sold, wasn't the money at your disposal? What made you think of doing such a thing? You have not lied to men but to God' (Acts 5:3, 4).

This states clearly that Ananias and Sapphira could have done anything they had wanted to do with their money. They did not have to give it to the church at all. But because they lied, not to men but to the Holy Spirit, judgment came on them.

The mere possession of things is not in itself the problem. The problem is that, being sinful men and women, we take what we are given and use it for ourselves at the expense of other people, rather than receiving these things as a gift in trust from God to be used in his service and at his direction. We need to learn that we are merely stewards of what God has given and must use what he has given rightly.

In the Sermon on the Mount, the Lord Jesus Christ was very explicit about this, saying that the problem is not the money itself but the desire to hoard it and use it selfishly. He commended what he called 'laying up treasures in heaven,' presumably by doing good works. 'Do not store up for yourselves treasures on earth, where moth and rust destroy, and where thieves break in and steal. But store up for yourselves treasures in heaven, where moth and rust do not destroy, and where thieves do not break in and steal. For where your treasure is, there your heart will be also' (Matt. 6:19, 20). Instead of hoarding wealth Jesus encouraged us to use it in God's service.

Our questions should not be 'How much can I make?' or 'How much can I spend?' We should ask rather, 'How much of a blessing can I be to others with the money God has entrusted to me?'

THE PROPER USE OF POSSESSIONS

In the passage from the Sermon on the Mount that I have just cited Jesus says four things about possessions. Since James had undoubtedly heard the Lord speak on this subject and had learned from him, he would certainly have echoed these teachings.

1. *Earthly riches are not lasting.* However valuable possessions may be in this life they will all pass away eventually. Possessions of every sort will perish. Therefore, our proper concern should be to store up spiritual wealth which does not perish. Jesus said, 'Do not store up for yourself treasures on earth, where moth and rust destroy, and where thieves break in and steal. But store up for yourselves treasures in heaven, where moth and rust do not destroy, and where thieves do not break in and steal' (Matt. 6:19, 20).

We know the uncertainty of riches. We talk about it all the time. In fact, in our day riches seem to be more uncertain than ever. Our culture is shouting the truth of Christ's statement. How foolish, then, exclusively to focus our attentions on and barter our lives for mere things!

2. *Possessions can control us rather than we controlling them.* Jesus suggests this point in the next verse, verse 21, saying, 'For where your treasure is, there your heart will be also.' This is the second thing we have to keep in mind: namely, either we will rule things or things will rule us, and if we fix our hearts on our earthly treasures, we will be bound by them. Several verses after this, in verse 24, Jesus makes this point again by referring to what the King James Version calls 'mammon'. The New International Version changed this to 'Money' (with a capital 'M') in order to make the

meaning more obvious, saying 'You cannot serve both God and Money.' But the word is actually 'mammon', and it has an instructive Hebrew origin.

It is interesting how the use of the word developed. Originally mammon was a positive term. It comes from a verb which means to entrust something to someone, that is, to give something to someone for safe-keeping. Usually, possessions, money or wealth was that which was entrusted. In spiritual terms this had a good meaning, too, because money is one thing God entrusts to us and is also by definition that which we entrust to other people to help them, when we give it to them or spend it on them. At this stage mammon had no bad connotations at all. To give it a bad connotation one had to put an adjective with it or add a qualifying noun. You had to say something like 'the mammon of unrighteousness' or 'the mammon of sin'.

What happened next is instructive. The active sense, 'to entrust', was changed to a passive meaning, namely, 'that in which one trusts'. So you can see what happens. At first, money is entrusted to us and is to be entrusted to other people to help them. When the active sense of the word predominates, the person who owns the money is in charge of it and is able to use it wisely and well. He or she is using the possessions. But when money comes to mean that in which one trusts, then the person involved is no longer using it or controlling it. Rather it is controlling that person.

At this point the word 'mammon', which was originally spelled with a small 'm', came to be spelled with a capital 'M', meaning that for such people Mammon had become a god. I have already pointed out that although the New International Version changes the word 'mammon' to 'money', presumably because the translators felt that no one today would understand what 'mammon' means, it nevertheless tries to capture the essential meaning of the verse by capitalizing 'Money'.

3. *Possessions are dangerous.* Jesus says something else about possessions in verses 22, 23: they are dangerous, because they tend to cloud one's spiritual vision. He says, 'The eye is the lamp of the body. If your eyes are good, your whole body will be full of light. But if your eyes are bad, your whole body will be full of darkness.'

William Barclay wrote of these verses: 'The idea behind this passage is one of childlike simplicity. The eye is regarded as the window by which the light gets into the whole body. The colour and state of a window decide what light gets into a room. If the window is clear, clean, and undistorted, the light will come flooding into the room and will illuminate every corner of it. If the glass of the window is coloured or frosted, distorted, dirty, or obscure, the light will be hindered and the room will not be lit up.... So then, says Jesus, the light which gets into any man's heart and soul and being depends on the spiritual state of the eye through which it has to pass, for the eye is the window of the whole body.'[1]

Do you see spiritual things clearly? Or is your vision of God clouded by spiritual cataracts or near-sightedness brought on by an unhealthy preoccupation with this world's things?

I am convinced that this is true for many Christians, particularly those living in the midst of western affluence. Now and then people like this complain to me that they cannot understand the Bible or that God seems far away. Or sometimes they are confused about the Christian life or about God's will for them. Well, it is not surprising in many of these cases, since that will always be so for one who knows his or her way around a supermarket or a brokerage house better than around the New Testament.

So remember, although Jesus did not speak against earthly

---

1. William Barclay, *The Gospel of Matthew* (Philadelphia: The Westminster Press, 1958), vol. I, p. 245.

wealth or possessions themselves, he did warn us against losing our spiritual vision because of them.

4. *You can only have one master.* The last point Jesus makes is that you cannot serve God and Money at the same time. Or, as James would say it, you cannot use your wealth as the wicked rich do and be a servant of the Lord Jesus Christ at the same time. The two are antithetical.

In one of his writings, Martin Lloyd-Jones tells the story of a farmer who came from the barn into the farmhouse. He was delighted. 'Our cow has just given birth to twin calves,' he said. He had been expecting only one calf, and he was so delighted about this unexpected bounty that he decided he would give one of them to the Lord. 'We are going to raise these two calves together, and one of them will be the Lord's calf and one will be our calf. When they grow old enough to sell, we'll sell one and give the proceeds to the church.'

His wife asked, 'Which one is the Lord's calf?'

He said, 'It doesn't matter. They are identical. We'll raise them together and then give the money from the sale of one to the Lord.'

The two calves seemed to be prospering, but one day the farmer came into the house with a long face.

'What's wrong?' his wife asked.

'The Lord's calf has died.'

She protested, 'What do you mean, "The Lord's calf has died"? You hadn't decided which one was the Lord's calf. How do you know it is the Lord's calf that died?'

'No,' he said. 'I always knew that the Lord's calf was the white one, and it is the white one that has died.'

The point is obvious. It will always be the Lord's calf that dies unless we get our priorities straight from the beginning. What we must recognize is that our possessions, whether they are many or few, are given to us by God and that we are only stewards of them, not owners. Therefore, we are to use these possessions under God's direction – not to bring glory to ourselves or to indulge ourselves, but to help other men and women.

9

THE LORD HELPS
THOSE WHO...
(James 5:7-12)

Be patient, then, brothers, until the Lord's coming. See how the farmer waits for the land to yield its valuable crop and how patient he is for the autumn and spring rains. You too, be patient and stand firm, because the Lord's coming is near. Don't grumble against each other, brothers, or you will be judged. The Judge is standing at the door!

Brothers, as an example of patience in the face of suffering, take the prophets who spoke in the name of the Lord. As you know, we consider blessed those who have persevered.

I have entitled this study 'The Lord Helps Those Who...' because it is suggestive since everyone knows how the sentence ends: 'The Lord helps those who *help themselves.*' We have other sayings that are similar to it. Perhaps you remember 'Praise the Lord and pass the ammunition.' It means, 'Praise God all you want, but don't forget to keep fighting. Trust God, but do your own part.'

When I think of those sayings, I think of some advice James gave his readers in the fifth chapter. We know that as a rule Christians are called to action. They are not to sit back and do nothing. If there is a battle to be fought, they are to lay hold of the ammunition and shoot it in the right direction. But suppose you cannot do that. Suppose you are one of the destitute, the downtrodden, the underprivileged of the world. Or suppose you are simply up against a force that is greater than you are.

James has advice for people like that, and his advice is twofold. He says, 'Be patient.' That is the first thing. Then, second, he says, 'Stand firm.'

PATIENCE IN SUFFERING

James has been talking about rich persons who oppress the poor. But then, having given a warning to the rich, he naturally turned his attention to the underprivileged – those the rich were oppressing. He told the rich not to oppress the poor. But since the rich will continue to oppress the poor anyway in most cases, what are the poor to do?

James tells them to be patient. He is not saying to be patient because there is nothing else they can do or to be patient because maybe the rich will treat them a little better if they are. No, he is saying, 'Be patient, remembering the God you serve.' When you remember that, you remember that the God you serve is a just God, that the Lord Jesus Christ, his Son, is returning in judgment, and the time is coming when the injustices that are being inflicted now will be made right. If we believe in this life only, that only what we have now is real, this argument would be worthless. But James is not talking to secularists. He is talking to those who believe in a future world and a sovereign God. Such people believe in justice, because God is a just God. So James says, 'If you are oppressed, be patient because in God's own time justice will be done.'

There is a story about an ungodly farmer in the midwest. He lived in a dominantly Christian community, and all the other farmers observed the Lord's Day and went to church on Sunday. This man's farm land was right across the road from the church. So to demonstrate his independence of religion he made it a point to plough his fields on Sunday mornings. While everyone else was singing praises to God, his tractor was going up and down the furrows and everyone could hear it. The summer went by. Harvest time came, and after the harvest this man wrote a letter to the newspaper explaining his position. He said, 'All summer long when the others were in church observing what they call the Lord's Day, I have been working in my fields. God has not punished me for my action. In fact, not only have my crops succeeded, but I've even been able to raise more crops than those who rested one day of the week. What do you say to that?' The editor of the paper, who must have been a Christian, printed the letter in full. But down at the bottom under this man's signature he added: 'God does not settle his accounts in October.'

This is what James is saying. We may undergo persecution; we may endure trouble; we may go through periods of distress; we may see the wicked prospering while we are suffering. But this is not the end of the matter. God will settle his accounts eventually.

However, James also talks about God judging Christians. This is because Christians have a human nature too, and because they easily think along lines that excuse themselves. They think, 'I am righteous; others are ungodly. Everything I do is right; everything they do is wrong.' So James directs a word to Christians, saying, 'And while you're at it, don't forget that the Judge of the ungodly is your Judge too, and that you also must give an answer to him one day. Make sure that your conduct is above reproach.'

STAND FIRM

Not only does James tell Christians to be patient, he also tells them to stand firm. Patience is a difficult virtue to achieve. There is a bit of worldly doggerel about patience that stresses this. It goes,

> Patience is a virtue, seize it if you can.
> Seldom found in woman, and never found in man.

One problem we have with patience is that it always appears to us to be passive, and we are usually activists. We suppose that if a person is to exercise patience, he has to sit quietly, hold his tongue, wait and trust that some day he will be vindicated.

That is not entirely true. Often we have to be patient in an active way. But whatever the case with patience, 'stand firm' suggests a more aggressive behavior. It suggests holding tightly to what you have. It implies bearing up under oppressions so that you might give testimony to the gospel, not retreating from what you know. 'Stand firm' means that we are to endure as the ambassadors of God. We are to make sure that we really live for him.

In the time of the apostle James, as well as in our own day, Christians could readily respond, 'Well, that's easy for you to say, so long as you're not suffering as I'm suffering. If you were suffering as I'm suffering, you couldn't say such things.' To answer such potential objections, James gives examples of the suffering of godly men in history and reminds his readers that they are enduring only what others have also known.

First, he directs their attention to the prophets. 'Brothers, as an example of patience in the face of suffering, take the prophets who spoke in the name of the Lord. As you know, we consider blessed those who have persevered' (vv. 10, 11). James does not name precisely which prophets he has in mind, but it is not difficult to guess. We think of the four great prophets – Isaiah, Jeremiah, Ezekiel and Daniel, each of whom suffered greatly for his profession. The great example is Jeremiah, who was terribly mistreated. Daniel's suffering is well known. The Book of Isaiah does not tell of Isaiah's suffering, but according to tradition, he was sawed in two for his faith. Perhaps this is behind the shocking incident referred to in Hebrews 11:37.

In the New Testament we think of Stephen and his martyrdom. Stephen gave his listeners a brief review of Jewish history, and as he got to the end he reminded them that there was not a messenger that God had sent who had not been rejected in his time: 'Was there ever a prophet your fathers did not persecute? They even killed those who predicted the coming of the Righteous One' (Acts 7:52). Of course, the Righteous One, the epitome and culmination of God's revelation, the messenger who was above all other messengers, was killed as well.

James is not encouraging us to seek persecution. But he is saying that if you endure suffering for the sake of righteousness, you should remember that it is not uncommon for God's people. All the prophets suffered. Are we to think that simply because we live in Britain or America we will not suffer for our profession of faith? When we take a stand upon God's teaching and attempt to live by that, contrary at times to the teaching or the drift of our culture, can we imagine that we will not suffer for it? Maybe God in his grace will spare us such things; but if they come, we are not to think that somehow God has suddenly abandoned us. 'No,' James says. 'Remember that it has happened to better men and women than you. Remember the prophets, and be sure that you stand firm, as they did.'

THE EXAMPLE OF RIGHTEOUS JOB

Although James does not mention what prophets he has in mind, as I said, he does mention one individual – not a prophet, so far as we know, but nevertheless one whose name is nearly synonymous with patient suffering: Job. Probably the reason James mentions Job is that in Job's case we have an outcome to the story, which James refers to. James has just said, 'Be patient in suffering because you have a righteous judge who will settle all things at the last day,' and although in the cases of Isaiah, Jeremiah and the others, God undoubtedly did settle the accounts, we do not know precisely what he did or how that happened, or even if there was any settling in this life. In the case of Job we have the outcome of the story.

We know that Job is an example of righteous suffering because, at the very beginning of the story, Job is called 'blameless and upright,' one who 'feared God and shunned evil' (Job 1:1). The statement does not mean that Job was sinless, but it does mean that he lived an upright life. Therefore, the suffering that came to him was not his own fault. Job had seven sons and three daughters. He was relatively rich. He had 7,000 sheep, 2,000 camels, 500 yoke of oxen, 500 donkeys. In addition to all this he had the servants to take care of those animals, and he had seven sons and three daughters.

The scene now shifts to heaven where we see the throne of God and are told that Satan and his hosts came to present themselves before God. God initiated the conversation by asking a question of Satan: 'Where have you come from and what have you been doing?'

Satan said, 'From roaming through the earth and going back

and forth in it' (v. 7).

Then God asked the really pertinent question, drawing attention to Job: 'Have you considered my servant Job? There is no one on earth like him; he is blameless and upright, a man who fears God and shuns evil' (v. 8).

I do not know whether Satan had established personal contact with Job before this or not. Satan is a created being. He is not omnipresent as God is. Therefore, he cannot be everywhere at once, and he may not actually have had contact with Job. But he had heard of Job, and his response showed this: 'Does Job fear God for nothing? [That is, "You have made him a rich man; why shouldn't a man serve you so long as you bless him with material things?"] Have you not put a hedge around him and his household and everything he has?' (vv. 9, 10).

The second half of that rejoinder is an interesting admission. For Satan is admitting that God had been protecting Job so that Satan had been unable to get to him. God sets a hedge around all his children, too. That part was true. However, the first part – the part about Job serving God only for what he could get out of it – was a slander.

To show that Job worshipped God for the sake of God alone and not for what God could do for him, God said, in effect, 'All right, let's lower the hedge a bit, just far enough for you to touch Job's possessions, but not his person.' Satan went out, rubbing his hands together in glee, thinking, 'This is what I've wanted all along. At last I'm going to get to that mealy-mouthed hypocrite. I'm going to make him curse God to his face.'

So disaster fell upon Job through Satan's agency. Servants told him, 'The oxen were ploughing and the donkeys were grazing nearby, and the Sabeans attacked and carried them off. They put the servants to the sword, and I am the only one who has escaped to tell you!' (vv. 14, 15).

While he was still speaking, a second servant arrived, who said, 'The fire of God fell from the sky and burned up the sheep and the servants' (v. 16).

A third messenger said, 'The Chaldeans formed three raiding parties and swept down on your camels and carried them off' (v. 17).

Finally, yet another messenger arrived. His message was the most dismal of all. 'Your sons and daughters were feasting and drinking wine at the oldest brother's house, when suddenly a mighty wind swept in from the desert and struck the four corners of the house. It collapsed on them and they are dead' (vv. 18, 19). In that one day all Job's possessions and family were taken from him. And Satan, who was looking on, stood back waiting for Job to curse God as he had predicted Job would do.

Job did nothing of the sort. Instead, he got up, tore his robes (an ancient symbol of mourning), shaved his head (also a symbol of mourning), knelt down and worshipped God, saying,

'Naked I came from my mother's womb,
and naked I shall depart.
The LORD gave and the LORD has taken away;
may the name of the LORD be praised'   (v. 21).

'In all this Job did not sin by charging God with wrongdoing' (v. 22).

The next scene is again back in heaven where Satan is presenting himself before God again. Again God asks, 'Where have you come from?'

This time Satan's answer seems a bit evasive. He does not mention Job, saying only, 'From roaming through the earth and going back and forth in it [as I always do]' (Job 2:2).

God probed further. 'Have you considered my servant Job?'

Satan knew what was coming, of course. He knew that God would ask him about Job, so he had his retort ready. Earlier he had said, 'Job worships you only because you have made him a rich man. You're good to him, so he is good to you.' But now he switches his argument, saying, 'The reason Job worships, loves and reveres you is not only because you take care of him — I'll grant you that — but because he is afraid of you and is concerned about his life.' His actual words were, 'Skin for skin! A man will give all he has for his own life' (v. 4). In other words, 'The reason Job doesn't curse you is because he is afraid that if he does, something even worse will come upon him.'

God said, 'All right, we'll lower the hedge a bit further. Now you can touch his person, but you cannot kill him.'

So Satan went out and afflicted Job with boils. In his misery Job sat among the ashes. Even his wife came to him and said, 'Curse God and die' (v. 9). But Job did not do it. He replied, 'Shall we accept good from God, and not trouble?' (v. 10).

The climax reads, 'In all this, Job did not sin in what he said' (v. 10). Job waited in patience and remained steadfast in what he knew about God, as James advised his readers to do so many years later.

THE END OF THE STORY

More lessons enter in at this point. Job's 'comforters' come, and they blame him for his sufferings. This was cruel. But they did one thing that most of us do not even bother to do. They at least sat down with Job, thus identifying with him in his misery. And they did not say anything for the first seven days! In other words, they did not consider that they had any right to speak to Job's condition at all, until they had first identified with him in his misery. We can be far worse than Job's comforters simply by saying to someone who is suffering, 'Oh, it's okay. Those things happen to everybody.'

Or 'God has done this to get your attention.' Or 'Well, maybe this is for the glory of God.' We must identify with suffering people first and only then will we have a right to speak to them.

Of course, when Job's comforters spoke, what they said was not really wise. They linked suffering to sin, which is true in one sense. But they argued that even if Job did not know what he had done, he must have sinned somehow. Or perhaps he did know and had been keeping silent about it for years. Maybe he had been putting up a front. Job knew this was not true. So he probably scratched his head, saying, 'I do not know what is happening. But there must be more to this than I understand.'

As the counsellors talked to him, Job replied argument by argument. He tried to reason it out, showing the fallacies of their counsel. Finally, when the counsellors had said everything they knew to say, Job was still left in his misery. He was no better off than before.

At this point, God intervened again.

Perhaps you think the story should end with God explaining everything to Job. Perhaps you think God should have said at this point, 'I've been waiting for these miserable counsellors to shut up so you could listen to what I have to say. I wanted them to exhaust their explanations so I could explain what is really happening.' But that is not what God does. On the surface it seems that the first thing God does is reduce Job to even deeper misery. All that Job has had to hang on to has been his knowledge of God. But now God says, 'Job, what do you really know anyhow? If you are going to understand my will and my ways, you have to begin with the fact that in your human knowledge you know next to nothing.'

God makes his point by asking a series of questions: 'Where were you when I laid the foundations of the world? Where were you when I hung the stars in the sky? Where were you when I made the winds? Where were you.... Where were you....' This goes on verse after verse and chapter after chapter, as God reminds Job of all these things that Job had probably never even thought about, let alone understood. Job must have been reduced to near nothingness.

Before, Job thought he understood things better than his friends, but now he recognized that he did not understand anything well at all. He was on the same level with them. So he prayed that God would work with them and forgive them for the abominable self-righteousness they demonstrated in their conversation.

Then, at the very end of the story, we are told that God made Job prosperous again (Job 42:10). God gave everything back to him double. He gave him 14,000 sheep, doubling the 7,000; he gave him 6,000 camels, doubling the 3,000; he gave him 1,000 oxen and 1,000 asses, doubling what he had previously owned in those categories.

Then there is something interesting. God gave Job seven sons and three daughters. He did not double them. Why? It is because when the animals were gone, they were really gone. They did not have imperishable souls. But when the sons and daughters were gone physically, they were not really gone. They were with God in heaven. They had been killed, but Job still had his original seven sons and three daughters, and God now gave him seven sons and three daughters more. In all this Job had triumphed.

This is what James is referring to, saying that when we suffer, we are to keep such truths in mind. God knows what he is doing. God does not do wrong. God is the righteous One, and those who live righteously, suffer patiently and stand fast will be rewarded by him properly at the last day.

10

PRAYER IS FOR WEAK PEOPLE
(James 5:13-20)

Is any one of you in trouble? He should pray. Is anyone happy? Let him sing songs of praise. Is any one of you sick? He should call the elders of the church to pray over him and anoint him with oil in the name of the Lord. And the prayer offered in faith will make the sick person well; the Lord will raise him up. If he has sinned, he will be forgiven. Therefore confess your sins to each other and pray for each other so that you may be healed. The prayer of a righteous man is powerful and effective.

There is a verse in this concluding section of James that has been a problem for many people, and we can easily understand why. It is the verse that speaks of anointing the sick with oil: 'Is any one of you sick? He should call the elders of the church to pray over him and anoint him with oil in the name of the Lord' (v. 14).

This verse has been interpreted in various ways. On the one hand, it has been used by the Roman Catholic Church as the basis for its sacrament of final or extreme unction. This fits well within the sacramental system of the Church of Rome, according to which grace is administered through the sacraments by a priest specifically commissioned to perform them. (This is the only text in Scripture that gives any support at all to that sacrament.) But it is certainly not the true meaning of the text. For the verse is not speaking of anointing a person just before he dies, but rather has in view the person's recovery. And it certainly is not a public but a very private act. That this is teaching the rite of final unction is a very mistaken interpretation.

On the other hand, this verse has been misinterpreted by Protestants who have seen it as a promise of healing for all Christians in all circumstances. Many healing services appeal to verses like this with the explanation that it is the birthright of every Christian to be healthy. And some even add to their argument that the word 'salvation' is based upon the word for health – *salud* (Latin) means 'health' or 'wholeness' – and argue, therefore, that when you are saved, you are entitled to the wholeness of your body as well as of your soul.

Well, God often does grant fullness of health, and sometimes he grants what seem to be miraculous healings. But nowhere in Scripture does God promise that health is the birthright of every Christian. The case of Job, whom we considered in our previous study, should dispel any such notions. Job suffered not only by the loss of his possessions and family but also by the loss of his health, and the sole reason for his suffering was that God might be glorified. Although God eventually restored him to health, health was certainly not his birthright, and he certainly did not suffer bad health because he lacked faith, as some of these teachers argue.

However, when we have dismissed these false interpretations, we still have the responsibility of determining what the verse means, and this is not easy to do.

B. B. Warfield in his book *Counterfeit Miracles* observed rightly that God does not always grant healings when oil is supplied and concluded that since God does not generally follow the sign by the reality, we ought to dispense with the sign until such times as God restores the reality. This is the way I personally approach the passage. But whether or not that is an adequate handling of the situation, I leave you to judge. Here I would only like to pursue this verse a bit further in the context of the chapter's total teaching.

ENCOURAGEMENT IN PRAYER

First, we need to see that James is talking not so much about anointing with oil or any other sacrament as about prayer. Indeed, the passage as a whole urges us to pray and encourages us in prayer. James says that God hears the prayers of the righteous. When the righteous pray, as Elijah did, God hears the prayer. Verse 16 says, 'The prayer of a righteous man is powerful and effective' ('The effectual fervent prayer of a righteous man availeth much,' KJV). We need to note carefully what this says and not read into it what it does not say. It does not say that the righteous man will get anything he prays for, including health. It only says that the prayer of a righteous person is efficacious. Therefore, the point and intent of the passage is encouragement.

What are we to say about that? We must say that when James encourages us to pray, it must be according to the rules God sets down for prayer. When the Bible talks about Jesus Christ, it is speaking about the true Christ. When the Bible speaks about the gospel, it is speaking about the true gospel. Similarly, when the Bible speaks about prayer, it is speaking about true prayer. All over the world men and women pray. Prayer is a part of every religion, but that kind of prayer is not what James is talking about.

What is it that makes prayer true prayer according to the Bible? Well, true prayer is prayer offered to the true God – to the God of the Old and New Testaments, the Father of the Lord Jesus Christ, and not the false gods of the heathen or even to other people.

In the Sermon on the Mount, just before Jesus gave that model of prayer that we call the Lord's Prayer, he spoke to people who had a tendency to pray ostentatiously. He referred to hypocrites who prayed on the street corners making a great display of piety, and he told his disciples, 'When you pray, go into your room, close the door and pray to your Father, who is unseen. Then your Father, who sees what is done in secret, will reward you' (Matt. 6:6). Obviously, our Lord was not speaking against prayer meetings, where two or three or more people meet together to pray. Nor was he saying that it is wrong to have prayer in public, as we do in a worship service. He meant, 'When you pray, make sure you are praying to God and not merely to other men and women.'

WHAT IS TRUE PRAYER?
True prayer can be defined as possessing these three elements.

1. *True prayer is prayer to God the Father.* Probably the single most important thing that can be said about prayer is that prayer must be offered to the God and Father of our Lord Jesus Christ and that when we pray, we must be certain that it is really to that God that we are praying. Sometimes when we kneel to pray, we instinctively go through a prayer ritual. We pray for certain things,

and we pray in certain ways; when we get to the end we say, 'Amen.' If someone asks us later in the day whether we prayed in the morning, we assure them that we certainly did pray; but if they ask us what we prayed for, we sometimes are not able to remember.

That is not really prayer in the full biblical sense. To do that we must pause and be conscious of the one to whom we are praying and not utter a word of prayer until we are sure that we are really in God's presence.

2. *True prayer is in the name of the Lord Jesus Christ.* Again, true prayer is prayer through the Lord Jesus Christ. This refers to the efficacy of Christ's death upon the cross where he shed his blood for our sins. The author of Hebrews encourages us 'to enter the Most Holy Place by the blood of Jesus' (Heb. 10:19). God is a holy God. Therefore, even if we would come to that God and pray to that God, we are unable to do so unless the way into the Most Holy Place is opened to us by the blood of Christ. We have no right of access to God on our own. We have no claim upon him. In fact, our sin is a barrier between ourselves and God. So when we come, we must be careful to come on the basis of what Jesus Christ has done on our behalf.

When you hear prayers given in public, quite often the name of Jesus is not even mentioned. Yet according to the Bible, a prayer like that is not a true prayer. God does not hear it, because it does not plead the blood of Jesus Christ as the basis upon which the prayer is to be heard and answered.

3. *True prayer is in the Holy Spirit.* Finally, we must say that true prayer is not only to God the Father and through the Lord Jesus Christ, but also in the Holy Spirit. This is taught in Ephesians 2:18, where we read 'through him we both have access to the Father by one Spirit.' That verse has the entire Trinity in it: 'the Father' is the

one to whom we pray; 'him' refers to Jesus, in whose name we pray; and it is in the power of the Holy 'Spirit' that we voice our petitions.

What do we mean when we say that we pray 'in' the Holy Spirit? This is a confession that we do not know how we should pray, and that we need the Holy Spirit to pray for us as we pray. We come to God with all kinds of requests, but how do we know that the things we are requesting are in accord with his will? How do we even know how to address God properly? How are we to plead for the things that lie upon our hearts? At this point the Spirit helps us, teaches us and interprets our prayers aright.

There is an interesting word in Ephesians 2:18, the word 'access'. It means 'an introduction'. It is used of the Holy Spirit in the sense that it is the Holy Spirit who introduces us to God in prayer. You know what it is like when you introduce Mary to John. You say, 'Mary, I'd like you to meet John. John works here in the city. He is an architect. He is interested in sky diving. And John, I'd like you to meet Mary. Mary hates sky diving, but she works in an architectural firm, as you do.' In an introduction you begin to tell each person a little bit about the other. That is what the Holy Spirit does. As we pray, the Holy Spirit opens the mind of God to us, so we might know him, and he directs us to make our requests to God properly.

So I summarize. True prayer is prayer to God the Father through the Lord Jesus Christ, that is, on the basis of his death, and in the power of the Holy Spirit.

'YOUR WILL BE DONE'

A second thing needs to be said about prayer: Prayer must be according to the will of God. The Bible has great things to say about prayer. Jesus said, 'You may ask me for anything in my name, and I will do it' (John 14:14). Somewhat later, John, who was there in the upper room and heard the Lord say this, wrote, 'Dear friends, if our hearts do not condemn us, we have confidence before God and receive from him anything we ask, because we obey his commands and do what pleases him' (I John 3:21, 22). If we put these two texts together we notice that Jesus said, 'Whatever you pray for you will get,' and John claims that this happened.

But notice also that when the Lord said, 'You may ask me for anything in my name, and I will do it,' he gave a condition. It is that we must pray 'in [his] name.' And John, when he says with great boldness that whatever he prays for, God does, explains that the condition under which this happens is: 1) to keep his commandments, and 2) do what pleases him.

People in Christian circles sometimes forget this. They read that if two or three agree on earth as touching anything, it will be done in heaven. So they get two or three Christian brothers and sisters together and say, 'Come on, I want you to pray with me about this thing. I want it to be done.' They pray and pray and pray. And when it is not done, they cannot understand why. They may even conclude that God does not keep his promises. That is nonsense, of course. God does keeps his promises, but he does so according to the conditions under which he makes the promises.

What does it mean to pray 'in the name of' Christ? It means to pray according to the will of Christ and in the manner of Christ, as Jesus himself would pray if he were in our circumstances. And when John says, 'because we obey his commands and do what pleases him,' he obviously means that as he studies the Word of God and finds out what God wants him to do, he does it. Furthermore, in addition to doing what he knows God's commands are, he seeks wherever possible, even in areas for which he does not have an explicit command, to do what he hopes will please his heavenly Father. When he does that, his prayers are answered, because they are according to God's sovereign and perfect will.

If somebody says, 'I am having a great deal of difficulty in my prayer life; I pray, but God doesn't answer my prayers,' the questions to ask are: Are you praying according to the will of God? Are you trying to keep his command? Are you obeying everything you know the Word of God requires? Are you seeking God's mind in order to please him? Prayer promises are given to people who do that.

We often use the phrase 'if it is your will' to save face. We pray, 'Lord, I very much want you to do such-and-such ... if it is your will.' But what we mean is: 'I suspect that it is not your will. So I am giving you an out. I am throwing in that phrase so that when you don't do what I ask you to do, you won't be embarrassed and neither will I.'

When Peter was imprisoned, the Christians in the home of Mary, the mother of John Mark, must have been praying that way. At least most of them were. For when God delivered Peter, they did not believe it. They must have been saying, 'Perseverance in prayer is important, so we must get together and pray.' They prayed all night, and that night, in the middle of the prayer meeting, God sent an angel to open the prison and let Peter out. Peter thought his Christian brothers and sisters might be praying for him, so he went to the house of Mary, where they were praying, and found the door locked. He knocked. Rhoda, the servant girl, answered. She opened the door a crack, saw Peter and went back to the prayer meeting, saying, 'You can stop praying now. Peter is here. He is knocking at the door.'

Do you know what happened? They responded, 'No, it can't be Peter. He's in prison. That's why we're praying?'

Rhoda insisted, 'He's at the door. I saw him. Do you think I would mistake Peter?'

Then they said, 'Well, then, Herod must already have killed him. It must be his ghost.' The knocking continued; there was no escaping it. So they went to the door, opened it, and Peter came in and told them how God had delivered him out of the prison (Acts 12:1-17).

You see, they were praying, 'if it be your will', but without faith that what they were praying for really was God's will. So they didn't believe it when it happened.

ANOINTING WITH OIL

Now let us come back to the matter of anointing with oil. Is James saying that oil or the process of anointing with oil by itself saves the sick? No, I don't think so. What James is doing is describing something that undoubtedly took place in his day. He was not prescribing a rite. He was not saying, 'I've got something new I want to tell you about. If anybody gets sick, here is what you are to do. First, you are to get some oil; then, you are to anoint your sick friend; then, you are to pray, and the anointing and prayer will heal him.' This is not what he was doing.

Oil was used in various ways in Judaism, often in the temple rites, and James must have had this in mind, since he is describing something that was normally done. He is saying, 'When you follow the normal procedure, make sure that you pray.' That is the emphasis. It is the prayer of faith which is effective by God's grace for healing.

To pray in faith is a response to God's revelation. Faith is hearing God and acting on the basis of what God says. So here we have the case of those who are assured in one way or another – perhaps subjectively, perhaps on the basis of their study of God's Word, perhaps because of some special circumstance – that God is going to do something for them and then, on the basis of that conviction and revelation, pray in faith that that very thing might be done. In such circumstances, James says, 'God who has, first of all, given the revelation, will, in response to the believing faith, do what he has promised.'

Certainly when he speaks of the effectual fervent prayer of a righteous man he is thinking in these terms.

Notice how James indicates that there are some to whom this does not apply. It does not apply to a backsliding Christian, a wayward Christian or a doubting Christian. It applies to a righteous Christian, who is living according to the commands of God and who is able to pray both effectively and fervently.

At that point we might say, 'Well, if that is the case, then I am certainly not going to be able to pray boldly. I doubt my righteousness. I know I'm not sinless. I sin daily in thought, word and deed. I hardly know how to pray. This must be for other people.'

James anticipated that objection, because in verse 17 he gives the example of the prophet Elijah, reminding us that Elijah was a man like ourselves. He had the same human weaknesses we have. After Elijah's great victory on Mount Carmel when the fire of God came down and consumed Baal's altar and all the prophets of Baal were taken away and killed, Jezebel warned Elijah: 'May the gods deal with me, be it ever so severely, if by this time tomorrow I do not make your life like that of one of them' (I Kings 19:2). Elijah was terrified. He ran away and hid. Obviously Elijah was sometimes weak and vacillating. Nevertheless, as James reminds us, he was a man who was used by God to speak spiritual words to King Ahab and bring judgment on that kingdom.

God told Elijah to tell Ahab that it would not rain, and it did not. The grass dried up; the crops withered; the animals began to die. The kingdom was devastated. Then, after three years, God sent Elijah to tell Ahab that it would rain again.

Elijah went up to Mount Carmel. He put his head between his knees in an attitude of prayer and sent a servant to the edge of the hill to look for some indication of rain. The boy returned and said, 'All I see is a broad expanse of the blue sky over the Mediterranean.'

Elijah said, 'Go look again.' The boy went back, and Elijah continued to pray. When the boy returned, Elijah asked, 'Did you see anything?' There was nothing. The sky was absolutely clear. Elijah sent the boy back seven times.

The seventh time the servant reported, 'A cloud as small as a man's hand is rising from the sea' (I Kings 18:44). Elijah knew that was it. So he said, 'Go and tell Ahab, "Hitch up your chariot and go down before the rain stops you"' (v. 44). Then he gathered his robes around himself and ran ahead, outdistancing the chariot. The rains came down, and the drought was broken.

James is reminding us how God worked through Elijah in that time. And he is encouraging us to be men and women of prayer – not men and women of presumption, who get an idea in their heads and baptize it by prayer, saying, 'This is what God is going to do,' when God had promised nothing of the sort. We are to be those who seek God's will and pray for it and thus become agents of the blessing God brings.

As James ends his book, he gives us a place to start. We usually want to start with something spectacular. We would like to pray for someone who is terminally ill and see that person get well immediately. Think how spiritual we could be! Well, there are times when God may operate like that, but James says that if we want to learn to pray, we should start at a place where we know that God wants to bless others: 'Remember this: Whoever turns a sinner from the error of his way will save him from death and cover over a multitude of sins' (v. 20).

Do you want to be a person of prayer? Begin by praying for sinners. Pray for those who need the gospel, because as God hears your prayer and saves those people, they will be rescued from death, and many sins that would have been committed by them in their lifetime will be averted.

STUDY
QUESTIONS

1

WHY DID GOD LET THIS HAPPEN?
(James 1:1-18)

1. Who was the writer of James?

2. Why do some Christians find James a somewhat difficult book to study?

3. What are some possible explanations for why things go wrong in our lives?

4. Which explanation is illustrated by the story of Job's sufferings?

5. How can we know which kind of suffering we are experiencing?

6. What must we always remember while we wait for God's answer to our 'why'?

2

I DON'T WANT TO BE A FANATIC
(James 1:19-27)

1. What is a fanatic?

2. How can a Christian properly be a fanatic according to James?

3. Can you list some examples of good 'fanatics' from the Bible, explaining how they meet the definition given?

4. Give some practical examples of how you can be fanatical in your faith.

5. What happens when we study the requirements of Christianity in the Scriptures?

3

MY FRIENDS ARE SPECIAL
(James 2:1-13)

1. What are some reasons we choose the friends we have?

2. Perhaps you can think of a person that you would like to have as a friend. Why does he or she appeal to you?

3. If you have ever found yourself showing favoritism to someone, how did you defend your actions before God?

4. How did Jesus confront this problem?

5. Who should be your friends?

4

SURE, I BELIEVE, SO WHAT?
(James 2:14-26)

1. What is the relationship between faith and works, and why is it so vital to our testimony?

2. These teachings in James can appear to be contradictory to Paul's epistles. How should we approach this problem, or any Bible problem?

3. Name five characteristics of false faith.

4. What are the characteristics of true faith?

5. How might God be calling you to exercise true faith in Christ today?

5

AT LEAST I'M NO HYPOCRITE!
(James 3:1-18)

1. What is the tongue problem?

2. To what practical illustrations is the tongue compared? How are they appropriate?

3. What is the solution to tongue control?

4. What is true wisdom? How does it contrast with worldly wisdom?

5. What have you learned in this chapter that will help you with your tongue problem?

6

IT'S HIS (HER) FAULT
(James 4:1-12)

1. Is 'The Lord helps those who help themselves' true or false? Why?

2. How can we be patient in suffering when we cannot help ourselves and no one comes to our aid?

3. James advises that the oppressed 'stand firm'. What examples from Scripture does he hold out for us to follow?

4. Job was not a prophet, but what can we learn from his experiences?

5. Was Job more spiritual than his friends? Should he have taken pride in his persecutions? Why or why not?

6. When God restored Job's possessions, he gave him double of all that he'd had, with the exception of his children. What is one explanation for this?

HOW MUCH INSURANCE DO I NEED?
(James 4:13-17)

1. What is the cause of so much of our unhappiness in life?

2. How can we control this problem?

3. Our self-seeking behaviour also leads to problems in our relationships with God. What is James' cure for this in verses 7 and 8 of chapter 4?

4. Describe the three types of temptations to which we are susceptible?

5. Set aside some time to discuss before the Lord anything that is troubling you. Ask him to show you if it is a problem caused from within you. Ask him if he can change you by changing your attitude toward someone else.

8

'BELIEVE ME, RICH IS BETTER'
(James 5:1-6)

1. What is the cause of so much of our unhappiness in life?

2. How can we control this problem?

3. Our self-seeking behaviour also leads to problems in our relationships with God. What is James' cure for this in verses 7 and 8 of chapter 4?

4. Describe the three types of temptations to which we are susceptible?

5. Set aside some time to discuss before the Lord anything that is troubling you. Ask him to show you if it is a problem caused from within you. Ask him if he can change you by changing your attitude toward someone else.

9

THE LORD HELPS THOSE WHO ...
(James 5:7-12)

1. What is the major flaw in preoccupation with future security?

2. What two great errors of judgment were the people James is describing guilty of making?

3. Describe the kind of planning that does fit with a committed Christian lifestyle.

4. James prescribes the help we need, starting with verse 15. Can you remember the three attitudes which should be characteristic of the Christian?

5. How do you measure up? Are you worried? Do you put God first in your planning? Are the talents he has given you being used for his glory, or yours?

10

PRAYER IS FOR WEAK PEOPLE
(James 5:13-20)

1. Why do some Christians feel entitled to good health as well as to salvation? Is their position substantiated by Scripture?

2. What was the origin of anointing the sick with oil when presenting prayers for their recovery?

3. Can you give three characteristics of true prayer discussed in this chapter?

4. What is another important element of prayer if we expect God to grant our requests?